Healthy VEGAN STREET FOOD

Healthy VEGAN STREET FOOD

JACKIE KEARNEY

PHOTOGRAPHY BY CLARE WINFIELD

SUSTAINABLE &
HEALTHY PLANT-BASED
RECIPES FROM INDIA
TO INDONESIA

RYLAND PETERS & SMALL
LONDON • NEW YORK

Senior Designer
Megan Smith
Editor
Kate Reeves-Brown
Art Director
Leslie Harrington
Editorial Director
Julia Charles
Head of Production
Patricia Harrington

Food Stylist
Emily Kydd
Prop Stylist
Hannah Wilkinson
Indexer
Hilary Bird

First published in 2022
by Ryland Peters & Small
20–21 Jockey's Fields,
London WC1R 4BW
and
341 E 116th Street,
New York, 10029

www.rylandpeters.com

10 9 8 7 6 5 4 3 2 1

Text © Jackie Kearney 2022
Design and photographs
© Ryland Peters & Small
2022

ISBN: 978-178879-470-1

US Library of Congress
Cataloging-in-Publication
Data has been applied for.

Printed and bound in China

Notes
· Both British (Metric) and
American (Imperial plus US
cups) measurements are
included in these recipes for
your convenience, however
it is important to work with
one set of measurements
and not alternate between
the two within a recipe.
· All spoon measurements
are level, unless otherwise
specified.
· Ovens should be preheated
to the specified temperature.
Recipes in this book were
tested using a regular oven.
If using a fan-assisted/
convection oven, follow the
manufacturer's instructions
for adjusting temperatures.
· When a recipe calls for the
grated zest of citrus fruit,
buy unwaxed fruit and wash
well before use. If you can
only find treated fruit, scrub
well in warm soapy water
and rinse before using.

Acknowledgements

First and foremost, I am forever grateful to my husband Lee
and our children Tevo and Roisin, who are always supportive
of my adventurous travel and writing endeavours, as well
as being the best recipe guinea pigs. This book would not
be what it is without the talented skills of Clare Winfield,
Emily Kydd, Megan Smith and Hannah Wilkinson, who
endeavoured to realize everything I imagined for this book
and more. I'm also indebted to my publishing team who
always give me incredible encouragement throughout
the process, and especially Kate Reeves-Brown, my ever-
patient and precise editor, Julia Charles for understanding
my vision and always lifting me up, Leslie Harrington,
Yvonne Dooley and Patricia Harrington.

I am thankful to Damien Lee, for being an inspirational
friend, who I am grateful to have known, even for a
short time. There are some wonderful people who have
supported me and taught me things on this book journey,
but special mention needs to go to Sarah Jones, a dear
friend I never expected to meet in these remote mountains,
fellow passionate cook, Mancunian and market lover.
Also Seema Gupta, Natalie Coleman, Urvashi Roe, Natalie
Rossiter, Mimi Aye and Charlotte O'Toole.

Picture credits

Travel photographs on the following pages by Lee James
and Tevo Kearney-James: 39 below right; 52; 61 below
left; 61 below right; 81 above left; 81 centre right; 100;
109 above right; 123 above right; 123 below left; 124;
129; 135; 142; 175 above right; 197; 202.

All other travel photographs by Adobe Stock: Endpapers
Niyaska; 14–15 Katyau; 17 above left ZoltanJosef; 17 above
right Oscar Espinosa; 17 below left Travel Wild; 17 below
right vmedia84; 23 Mazur Travel; 30 Mubarak; 39 above
left Em Campos; 39 above right Danny Ye; 39 below left
Aliaksei; 39 centre right Marbenzu; 56 Zah108; 59 Lovina;
61 above left Olga Khoroshunova; 61 above right Ivan; 61
centre right efesenko; 70 subjob; 78–79 katyau; 81 above
right Jesse; 81 below right Galyna Andrushko; 86 Photo
Gallery; 105 visitr; 109 above left andrii_lutsyk; 109 below
left Khamhoung; 109 below right bennnn; 113 PixHound;
123 above left sabino.parente; 123 centre right cristaltran;
123 below right montecellllo; 136 Steve Lovegrove; 137
Marion; 145 Juliane Franke; 152–153 Niyaska; 155 above
left vanzyst; 155 above right Chee-Onn Leong; 155 below
left Alexey Pelikh; 155 centre right Wirestock; 155 below
right Elena Ermakova; 170 jahmaica; 172 Artorn; 175 above
left Michael; 175 below left Belikova Oksana; 175 centre
right Ekaterina Pokrovsky; 175 below right De Visu; 178
R.M.Runes; 203 Brent Hofacker.

Contents

Welcome to Healthy Vegan Street Food

When I first wrote *Vegan Street Food*, I remember my publisher asking me where I saw the book's position, in travel or in food? It's still a challenging question for me, as so much of the food I love is inspired by and intrinsically connected to travel, and especially the street food and café culture across the subcontinent and South-East Asia. For me, it's this connection to travel that gives food this kind of power to transport us back to these experiences and moments from journeys and destinations where we lost and found ourselves in some way.

For those readers familiar with *Vegan Street Food*, you will already know about my committed passion for family travel. Since I wrote that book, neither that, nor my love of street food, has dwindled. There are no repeat recipes in here, but there are certainly more travel stories. From our gap year and extended trips, when the twins were under 10, to more adventures when they were teens and young adults, we have spent more than two years travelling as a family in Asia, mostly overland. And when I realized I had spent more than one per cent of my life in Indonesia, it made me smile deeply and reminded me that one day I may still move to that Lombok hillside.

For now I'm happy to stay closer to my family in Europe, but my dining table is devoted to the variety of flavours and culinary inspiration from street food and café culture across Asia.

Why healthy vegan street food?

In my teens, I became a vegetarian because I didn't want to eat animals. It was that simple for me at that time. Factory farming was rife and, with limited alternatives, it felt incongruous to consume meat alongside my deep love for all creatures great and small. By the time I reached my 30s and 40s, our environmental knowledge base had grown so rapidly and, like many others, I leaned more and more towards plant-based food. Today, it is a deeply politicized topic, but this is also a time where we recognize the importance of individual wellness and what we can do to take better care of ourselves, as well as the environment around us.

In early 2020 I started working with noodle company entrepreneur, and five-times cancer warrior, Damien Lee. Working with someone so passionately committed to eating well, I fell under Damien's inspirational spell and we successfully published his noodle company cookbook. Tragically Damien passed away in early 2021, shortly before publication. His impact on my life will stay with me through his dedicated passion for making food that can help make us stronger, especially if our bodies are fighting other battles. Sadly as we age, this becomes a bigger feature in our lives.

There are some simple, unequivocal facts about aging. We become more prone to diseases that are considered characteristic, such as cardiovascular (heart and circulatory health), dysmetabolic (such as diabetes), autoimmune (such as thyroid problems), neurodegenerative (such as Alzheimer's) and oncological (cancers). Researchers now recognize that we can develop more inflammatory responses as we age. Together with – often chemically driven – intensive farming, this might offer an explanation as to the growth of autoimmune conditions and cancers, both of which are considered to be inflammatory responses within the body.

There's also a growing body of research on gut health, the importance of maintaining a healthy microbiome and the crucial connections to our overall well-being. Our gut is now considered to be one of the principal organs of the body, and yet more than one in 10 of the UK population, and up to 15 per cent of Americans, are diagnosed with gut-related disorders. The impact of this on population well-being is difficult to calculate, but as someone who has been managing an autoimmune disease for more than a decade, I know the fallout across our physical and mental health can lower life quality.

There's also a plethora of data out there that explains the complexities of the glycaemic index (how our bodies respond to sugars), why not all carbohydrates are created equal and that how we eat them is vitally important. I grew up during the era of low-fat diets, and it took several years for me to understand that healthy fats are essential to our health. Eating healthy fats and protein helps us consume carbohydrates without spiking our blood sugar, as well as satiating our hunger for longer. As I experienced severe fluctuations in my health, I became focussed on understanding more about the foods I need to eat more of, and the potential inflammatory effects of certain foods (obviously this isn't something that affects everyone). All this information can actually become quite overwhelming, and even more so when deciding what's best to eat.

What should we be eating?

Wholefoods and mostly plants is a great mantra to aim for. If we eat like this for most of the time, we're likely to have a positive impact on our overall health. The scientific data is unequivocal. A wholefood plant-based diet is the most healthful thing you can do for your well-being. This has been proven time and time again across numerous studies. However, vegan food is not always healthy. There is a huge global trend for highly processed and vegan junk food (which is often packed with salt, sugars and bad fats, whilst lacking in protein, healthy fats and essential nutrients) and this has led many down a path that could well lead to future health problems. When eating plant-based, or any kind of diet to be fair, it's crucial to understand what we need to fuel ourselves in the best way possible for the lives we lead, and to meet our own individual needs. Eating a rainbow of food to fulfil our essential nutrient needs is an easy way to envision a healthful plate of food. Including regular intakes of raw foods that are naturally packed with prebiotics and probiotic fermented foods, such as kimchi, sauerkraut and cultured yogurt, can also support our gut health and overall well-being. There are nutrients that can be more challenging to include and absorb when you eat purely vegan, so it's also essential to be aware of where those gaps can occur. Including additional amino-rich foods (such as using coconut aminos) or additional supplements is helpful.

Just to be clear here, food is not actual medicine. As a former health researcher and academic, and someone who has also tried to 'cure' my own autoimmune disease through diet, I'm solidly in the camp of science. When I've had a thyroid storm, it's medication not food that has prevented me from dying. But having an autoimmune disease has also taught me that we can affect our overall well-being through what we consume. What we eat, along with exercise, stress management and sleep, is recognized as a powerful directive on our well-being. We can radically shift our health status and longevity through diet, yet functional/integrative medicine remains mostly isolated and under-utilized by mainstream health care.

Delicious travel

It is delicious food that is the focus of this book. I have spent some time here talking about the health research and impetus behind why I wanted to write this book, but let's not get lost in that quagmire of often confusing and contradictory recommendations. My passion is still very much focussed on the street food of Asia. I love street food now as much as I always have. And I'm still as besotted with the complex and diverse flavours of the Indian subcontinent and South-East Asia. No matter how often I travel, the opportunity to enjoy new dishes is always there. As I started to adjust my diet to a healthier approach, I sought out and adapted recipes that aligned with how I wanted to eat, with a focus on the right kind of produce. So much of Asian street food and home cooking is naturally healthful and adaptable to plant-based eating.

Living in these rural Italian mountains has certainly made me rethink how I go about creating great flavours with less access to such diverse ingredients. Making things simpler just feels like the most likely route to sustaining healthy eating. Because I rely on cooking from scratch on a daily basis, it curbed my inclinations for lengthier recipes (although not entirely!). Living in Italy, there are also several months of the year where it's just too damn hot to be hanging out in the kitchen all afternoon, so I needed some low-prep recipes and, of course, some flavourful raw dishes, too. Of course I still

enjoy a fine vegan banquet from time to time. There's a diverse range of recipes within this book, from the super simple to the more complex, and they reflect many of the authentic flavours of vibrant street-food and café classics, alongside my own healthy and accessible adaptations.

I have always felt healthier and stronger when I've been travelling in Asia. Eating fresh food made with produce that hasn't travelled too far and is high in wholefood content obviously plays a large part in this. Like my first book, this too is a celebration of the often naturally vegan food that is readily accessible across Asia. From street-food stalls to roadside cafés, these recipes are inspired by my extensive travels with my family, as well as the solo trips I've taken to explore the growing wellness culture and tourism in the Indian subcontinent and South-East Asia.

There's a natural alignment between this wellness industry and many of the cultural practices in these countries. From the ancient ayurvedic and yogic teachings in the subcontinent to the meditation and mindfulness practices across South-East Asia. Some might object to the diversion from the wholly traditional, but I don't believe this is a valid critique. Like anywhere in the world, the growth, change and adaptation that builds upon the old and incorporates the new is an integral part of modern Asian food. For me, the street food of Asia is the perfect starting point for rapid adaptation to new knowledge, with adaptable ingredients that are intrinsically linked to seasonality and abundance. So much of this food is healthful, plant-based and naturally gluten-free, whereas so much Western food is centred around wheat, which is, sadly, used to bulk out our plates in place of fresh, healthful veggies and protein.

Through the lens of a traveller

As a former published sociologist, I'm not going to shy away from facing some important issues and questions that are raised here. I am a white woman writing about a small aspect of Asian food. The knowledge I've gained is through the lens of a traveller, the incredibly generous people I've been fortunate enough to meet on the way, my Manchester roots (so intertwined with subcontinent cultures), and my friends and peers. Our journeys through Asia have been those of white, privileged travellers, who've been afforded the circumstance, social capital, mobility and finances to pursue this. It's something I have considered deeply over the years, in relation to the plethora of issues I've experienced, observed and played a part in. We have left places because we have known that simply by being there, we could be contributing to local harm.

That being said, I have made choices in my life about where I wanted to be and the kind of life I wanted for my family. I have always been a traveller, in my heart and mind and actions; in the choices I made about the kind of work I did. I chose less well paid jobs with no security that offered me gaps between contracts to pursue extended trips; because of that I've spent nearly three years of my life in India, Sri Lanka and South-East Asia.

We choose to stay in a lot so we can save up for our next big adventure; it took three years to save for our family gap year. And I do a lot of research. We try to be mindful about the journeys we take and where we stay. This doesn't always go to plan, of course. Many places on the 'travellers trail' can lead you to white-dominated hell holes, where foreigners have imposed their own culture onto fragile local environments – for example a tiny Laos village that has started to resemble an Ibizan party town. We left, obviously. Or that time I accidentally stayed in the heart of a city red-light district on my own, so I immersed myself in reading essays about imperialism, the portrayal of Orientalism and how it relates to sex work. I read a Jodi Picoult novel, too. But my point is, we can choose to educate ourselves about our whiteness, about history, about white imperialism/colonialism and thus make more informed choices. Reading histories and local biographies is a great way to gain more insight and understanding of local cultures. In my opinion, no one should visit somewhere like Cambodia or Burma without reading a history book and at least one biography from someone who survived the Khmer Rouge or Myanmar Junta. And don't even get me started on why we don't learn about Indian partition in British schools.

If you're a travel foodie like me, I highly recommend reading more comprehensive speciality cookbooks by authors of East and South-East Asian heritage, who can share their stories and experiences first-hand. This is why I buy all kinds of cookbooks, vegan or not. I buy cookbooks when I'm travelling, sometimes written in other languages. I want to learn about the home kitchens of their childhoods, and understand more about the important role that food plays in their cultures, as well as supporting East and South-East Asian writers and their small businesses. See page 208 for a small sample of some recommendations.

Travel and tourism are crucial to Asian economies. The economic impacts of the Covid-19 pandemic are severe, but we can choose to educate ourselves and make better choices about where and how we travel. It is definitely time for tourists to return. The devastation to the travel and tourism industry as a result of this pandemic is vast. Sadly one of the negative fallouts of this has been an increase in xenophobia and racism. Like the world over, it is small business owners and workers who have suffered the most. But as the world reopens, it is time for those of us who love to travel to stride out into the world again, explore, meet and eat. And in-between growing food and building our Italian retreat, you might just find me back on that Lombok hillside.

Ingredients

This section is about store-cupboard dietary advice for healthier choices, rather than a step-by-step catalogue for spices and herbs, as most of these are fairly well known and accessible these days. There is also a good guide to store-cupboard spices in *Vegan Street Food*. Here I will introduce some of the key ingredients I recommend across many recipes in this book, and explain some of the reasons why these substitutions may assist you in eating more healthily.

I have already mentioned that people who eat solely plant-based diets need to be mindful about certain nutrients, and the best combinations to eat them in. For example, plant-based proteins need to be eaten alongside essential amino acids (EAAs), such as leucine, which are the building blocks for protein. These are less available in plant-based foods. Some high-protein sources, such as pumpkin or squash seeds, are missing essential EAAs like lysine, and pea protein lacks methionine and cysteine. Soya beans/soybeans are the best source of all for EAA profile and protein, better than several meat sources in fact. White beans, peas, quinoa and cashew nuts are also all very good sources of EAAs.

Plant-based proteins

Most recipes in this book include a healthy portion of plant-based protein. An essential macro in our diets that helps build muscle, stabilizes insulin and can improve metabolic health whilst satiating hunger for longer.

There are a variety of plant-based proteins available to us, an especially good source being soya beans/soybeans and, of course, tempeh and tofu. The latter being the most processed of the three. Wheat gluten, also known as seitan, is one of the biggest sources of protein, however I have my doubts about whether this is the healthiest protein for people to be eating in very large quantities, as gluten can have an inflammatory effect for some people, and not only for coeliacs/celiacs. There are many other autoimmune diseases that respond well to removing or reducing gluten consumption, including rheumatic and thyroid diseases. Non-coeliac/celiac gluten sensitivity is a muddy area of research and clinical understanding. However, as someone with an autoimmune disease that has responded well to removing gluten from their diet, I believe the jury cannot return a conclusive verdict on this matter at this time. Therefore, the decision to eat gluten can only be decided at an individual level, and, even better, under the guidance of a qualified dietitian or functional medicine doctor.

Other good sources of plant-based protein include beans, nuts and seeds (especially hemp seeds, linseeds/flaxseeds and chia seeds). If using dried beans, I recommend using a pressure cooker to prepare them after soaking, so that you can ensure all traces of lectins have been destroyed. Soaking nuts and seeds before using activates the enzymes, breaking down phytic acid and enzyme inhibitors, and thus making their nutrients more available to our bodies. Another popular protein source is mycoprotein, which is used to make Quorn products. There are increasingly more mock meat products, such as vegan meatballs and sausages made with pea protein. Pea protein is a great alternative to gluten flour for making mock meats.

For recipes in this book, and much of my cooking, I always keep several accessible options in the fridge and freezer, including tofu/beancurd (fresh, dried, firm and silken), tempeh, pea protein mock meatballs, soya/soy or Quorn mock chicken, and plenty of protein-rich veggies like broccoli, leafy greens and mushrooms.

Liquid aminos

As mentioned already, along with healthy proteins, we need essential amino acids. One of my favourite sources of EAAs is coconut aminos, a natural wholefood alternative to soy sauce made from coconut sap, nectar, garlic, sugar and salt. This umami-rich sauce can be used instead of soy sauce or tamari. Liquid aminos is also made from soya beans/soybeans, in a different wheat-free process to soy sauce. Like tamari, liquid aminos is naturally gluten-free, and contains 16 of the essential and non-essential amino acids we need, as well as trace minerals and vitamins C and B complex. Anything that bumps up your B12 is always a good idea for plant-based eaters, too (hence the popularity of fortified nutritional yeast amongst vegans). Like MSG, liquid aminos contains glutamate, giving it that mouth-watering quality. Liquid aminos contains 75 per cent less salt than traditional soy sauce. So all in all, it's a very easy, healthy win. Of course, you can still use soy sauce (there are lower salt versions available now) or use tamari for a naturally gluten-free option, as these are both more widely available. Kikkoman is the industry standard. Coconut aminos is more difficult to find in supermarkets but can be sourced online. My preferred brands are Coconut Secret and Bragg's (made using soya/soy).

Wholegrains & complex carbs

There are lots of naturally gluten-free wholegrains featured in the recipes here. These include quinoa, millet, buckwheat and black, red and wholegrain rice, as well as alternatives to white rice noodles (which I still love and include here), such as mung bean, sweet potato and even riceberry noodles. These are a new favourite of mine along with other rice wholegrains. They are very popular in healthy Thai and Indonesian cafés. In recent years I've been enjoying all kinds of wholefood, higher protein and lower carb noodles, such as soya bean/soybean, konjac and even matcha and buckwheat. I also eat vegetable noodles (such as courgetti/zoodles). Ancient grains like teff, amaranth and farro can be used instead of rice, although farro is not gluten-free.

It's important to eat a variety of wholegrains, especially if eating less or no gluten, because a large reduction in grains will reduce crucially important dietary fibre (something very few people eat enough of already). Low-carb diets can lower dietary fibre, which can contribute to increasing the risks of diabetes, cardiovascular disease and cancer. Dietary fibre is high in antioxidants, anti-inflammatory and essential to gut health. If we eat fewer gluten-filled grains, it's important to eat plenty of wholefood alternatives, as well as cooking with fresh fibre-rich vegetables like leafy greens and broccoli.

Healthy fats

There are lots of vegetable fats available these days, and they vary greatly in their health benefits. After the confusing dietary messages of the 70s and 80s, encouraging us to eat a low-fat diet, we now understand that healthy fats are essential for health.

But what is a healthy fat? Monosaturated and polyunsaturated fats contain plenty of omega-3 fatty acids, the key to every cell structure in our bodies and essential to cardiovascular, neurological and immune system health. However, whilst some polyunsaturated fats are really good for us, not all are stable at higher cooking temperatures. These less-stable oils, such as olive oil, oxidize quickly to form free radicals and harmful compounds. Unrefined olive oils are best used at lower cooking temperatures, in dressings or at the end of the cooking process. Soya bean/soybean, corn/maize, sunflower/safflower and even rapeseed/canola oils all start to oxidize at higher temperatures, despite the fact they are sold as frying oils. Whilst rapeseed oil, or the modified Canadian and US version canola oil, do have a much higher smoke point, they are less stable polyunsaturated fats, so they break down and produce higher levels of free radicals.

Monosaturated fats are the most stable for cooking. The most stable oil for frying is avocado oil, which is a healthy but expensive option. The next best option for high-temperature cooking is coconut oil, which is very stable. However, like any saturated fat, it should be used in moderation. Saying that, coconut oil is very different from saturated animal fats, as it is an MCT oil (contains a high level of medium-chain triglyceride fatty acids) and is said to support gut health and cognitive performance. I recommend using a culinary/unflavoured coconut oil for most higher temperature cooking, as it is affordable and can be used in smaller amounts. Most seed or nut oils will have a higher burning temperature too (less of those nasty free radicals), so it's useful to keep a good-quality oil like this in the cupboard: try sesame (toasted bringing its own flavour to the party) or highly nutritious mustard seed (which I use to make tempering for dals and curries). Pomace or light olive oil, which is processed from the olive stone, is a good option, too.

Healthier sugars

Nutrition science is still in its infancy, but if there's one fact that most agree on, it is simply that sugar is generally bad for our health. Some say it is more addictive than cocaine. As a former substance misuse researcher, I don't know about that claim, but it's clear that our glycaemic response is best kept at a stable rate, and spiking our insulin could lead us into a variety of health problems (and may potentially shorten our life span). The best natural plant-based sweeteners to use are date syrup or raw maple syrup, both of which contain some additional nutrients and have a lower glycaemic index than processed or refined sugars. Coconut sugar is also a good option, and I find that due to its sweetness, it's quite possible to use less in a recipe

than refined sugar. When eating something higher in sugar, it helps to eat this alongside protein, as this stabilizes the insulin response. You will find dessert recipes in this book that are protein-packed as well as being a sweet treat. I always have plenty of raw cashews, walnuts, blanched almonds and desiccated/dried unsweetened shredded coconut at the ready in my cupboard, as well as some high-quality vegan dark/bittersweet chocolate.

VEGAN FISH SAUCE

Useful vegan cooking condiments include good-quality soy sauce or gluten-free tamari, toasted sesame oil, Korean fermented soya bean/soybean paste or doenjang, brown or red miso paste, rice vinegar, dark soy sauce or vegan oyster sauce (sometimes called stir-fry or mushroom sauce), sambol olek or other chilli/chili sauce, tamarind pulp or paste and seaweed seasoning. You can also now buy vegan fish sauce online and in some Asian supermarkets. Or you can make your own. This recipe has been re-shaped a little since its first appearance in Vegan Street Food.

2 tablespoons seaweed, such as dulse
2 dried shiitake or porcini mushrooms
1 teaspoon sea salt
3 tablespoons coconut aminos,
   or use soy sauce (or tamari for gluten-free)
2 teaspoons brown or red miso paste

Add the seaweed and dried mushrooms to a small pan with 375 ml/1½ cups water, and place over high heat. Bring to the boil, then reduce the heat and simmer for 15 minutes.

Remove from the heat and let stand for 20 minutes. Pour the liquid through a fine sieve/strainer, squeezing out all the juices from the mushrooms (reserve for another recipe). Add the salt, coconut aminos and miso paste. Mix well. Store in a sterilized bottle for up to 1 month in the fridge.

INDIA &
SRI LANKA

Northern India

India is at the top of my list of places to return to as the world reopens for travel. Six months of overland travel has barely scratched the surface for me and I'm keen to spend some time in an ashram at some point in my life. Our journey as a young family took us from the northern most borders with Pakistan, zigzagging across the country for six months until we reached Sri Lanka. Whilst we spent several months in Sri Lanka (and Nepal) a few years later, we have yet to return to India. Fortunately my home town of Manchester is one of India's many heart homes for food, especially Punjabi cuisine.

After the initial shock of landing in Delhi during the worst storms in 50 years, the children were distracted from the flooded streets by the vibrancy. Beautiful colours covered temples, decorative gateways and people's clothing. Even religious pop-ups like the tent outside our guesthouse was adorned with garish and garlanded statues of gods, a gravity-defying chandelier and a giant mechanical peacock.

We started our overland trip from the northernmost region of Ladakh, nestled high in the Himalaya and sandwiched between northern Pakistan and a sliver of Afghanistan on one side, and Tibet and the remote north-west Chinese province of Xinjiang on the other. We spent a few weeks acclimatizing to our new life on the road. The children tackled treks that many adults would find challenging, growing out of two pairs of hiking boots during the trip and eating with locals without batting an eyelid. To be fair, it was me and Lee whose bodies took more time to adjust – to the altitude, the food and the battering that overland travel can give you.

Each leg of our Indian journey wowed us in some way or another. We got lost in ancient times, trekking in the ethereal and stark landscapes of Ladakh, learning about Buddhist culture and practices and talking to Tibetan refugees about their lives and hopes for the future. We then spent several weeks criss-crossing the often precarious and ever-shifting roads of Himachel Pradesh, with softer mountain-scapes of dense green forest, like pinched green scatter cushions on a backdrop of snowy rugged peaks. All the while reintroducing ourselves to more populous places again, and learning about the history of partition as we travelled. We all read vociferously. The children, aged seven at the time, returned to the UK with reading ages of 16 year olds.

The daily sunset closing ceremony at the Attari (Pakistan) and Wagah (India) border has become a major attraction over the years, and, consequently, large banks of concrete seating have been erected. We were crammed into the Indian side with thousands of spectators, mostly all pumped for a big party! We sat next to a group of day-trippers from Delhi. The young men had to catch the last train back to the capital, so I suspect it was rowdier carriage than usual that night. The Pakistan contingent numbered about eleven as far as we could see, so we can only assume they have better things to do than watch the Pakistan Rangers annihilate the Indian Border Security Force with their high-leg and wobble-shake-thrust moves. It's certainly a spectacle for the newcomer, and there is plenty of snacking to be had in this almost-festival atmosphere.

Northern India introduced us to many extremes, from extreme altitude to depths of poverty that taught us all many lessons in gratitude. I had great intentions to visit several yoga retreats, from Manali to McCleod Ganj, but sadly illness got in the way. It wasn't until Goa that I got to take part in some incredible yoga practice that sowed some seeds about what I'd like my future to look like.

From the Punjab and western borders of Pakistan, we took trains further east via more favourable stops in Delhi, up to the north-east regions from Lucknow and holy Varanasi to the ancient city of Patna, where the region of Bahar pushes temptingly close to the foothills of Sikkim (another ancient Buddhist region we had hoped to visit, but winter had finally come). We joined in the celebrations of Dusshera in the north and Diwali in Varanasi. Only very occasional encounters on our journey had us concerned. We were more often embraced with much loving kindness and generosity in every village, town and city – from the second-most-northern city of Leh in Ladakh to the southernmost tip of Kerala, and crossing the width of the country on the longest train journey of

our lives. And on rare occasions, if all else failed us, there was always impeccable food to be had. It would be impossible to name our most memorable meal in India. There were simply too many.

Clockwise from top left: Buddhist prayer flags on the mountain pass, Leh, Ladakh; Flower garland adorning Ganesha, the elephant-headed son of Shiva and Parvati; Diwali celebrations along the banks of the River Ganges, Varanasi, Uttar Pradesh; Chapati wallah at a Manali street market, Himachel Pradesh.

HIMALAYAN ENERGY BARS

I'm terrible at breakfast in a traditional sense. I've never been one to eat until I'm actually hungry, so I end up naturally intermittently fasting. When I was young, so many adults would scold me for this, even when I tried to explain that milk made me feel unwell. Breakfast is the most important meal of the day, they would say. Well, it turns out they were wrong. I am actually lactose-intolerant, and intermittent fasting is good for insulin resistance. Having stable blood sugar is important for a healthy system. However, when we extend our intermittent fast beyond breakfast, it's easy to fall into the trap of sudden hunger and grabbing something that's less nutritionally dense. I learned on many retreats, and from my Indian fasting friends, that nutrient density is essential when 'breaking fast', whether fasting intermittently or for several days.

I make these bars for our retreat guests who like to hike up our local mountains and adventure into the wilderness. The perfect backpack snack! They are nutritionally balanced, full of energy, high in iron and vitamin C (a very important combination for vegans and vegetarians), high in good fats and boast a decent hit of protein.

120 g/1 cup cashew nuts

90 g/⅔ cup walnut halves

140 g/generous 1 cup whole skinless almonds

75 g/½ cup pumpkin seeds, soaked and roughly chopped, or use sunflower seeds

25 g/scant ¼ cup pitted dates, finely chopped, or use dried mulberries

100 g/1⅓ cups desiccated/dried unsweetened shredded coconut

60 g/⅔ cup goji berries, or use dried mulberries

2½ tablespoons date syrup, or use pure maple syrup or unrefined coconut sugar

1 tablespoon chia seeds, soaked in 2 tablespoons water

½ teaspoon salt

1 teaspoon vanilla bean paste, or use vanilla extract or seeds of ½ vanilla pod/bean

30 x 20-cm/12 x 8-in. baking tray/ sheet pan, lined with parchment

MAKES 14

Preheat the oven to 165°C (325°F) Gas 3.

Place half the cashews, walnuts and almonds into a food processor or blender and lightly blitz. Place the remaining nuts onto a chopping board and roughly chop. Put the blitzed and chopped nuts into a large bowl and add all the remaining ingredients. Using your hands, mix everything really well.

Tip the mixture onto the lined baking tray/sheet pan. Using the back of a spoon, gently press the mixture into the pan and spread it evenly.

Bake in the preheated oven for 20–25 minutes until just golden brown.

Allow to cool completely before turning out onto a chopping board and peeling off the paper. Using a sharp knife, cut into 14 small bars. The bars will keep for up to 1 week in an airtight container.

HARA BHARA GREEN CUTLETS *with cashew cachumba chaat*

If I still had a street food menu, I'd definitely serve this dish. These little green beauties are naturally vegan and gluten-free, and packed with nutritious greens. You can reduce the spicing of the cutlets for younger palates. Chaat salads are a great way to wake up your raw food, and can be sprinkled on lots of other dishes. This little chaat salad is adaptable to most nuts and salad veg – try walnuts and ceviche courgette/zucchini (dice extra small and marinate in citrus for 20 minutes). Buy pomegranates in season, and pop the seeds in the freezer.

150 g/1 cup fresh or frozen peas
150 g/3 cups spinach, or use 175 g/
   1 cup frozen spinach, or substitute
   other dark leafy greens like chard or kale
½ teaspoon cumin seeds (optional)
2–3 heaped tablespoons gram flour
   (chickpea/garbanzo bean flour)
5-cm/2-in. thumb of fresh ginger, peeled
   and finely chopped, or use 2 heaped
   tablespoons ginger paste
1–2 green finger chillies/chiles, finely
   chopped, or use 1 scant teaspoon dried
   chilli flakes/hot red pepper flakes
1–2 tablespoons culinary/unflavoured
   coconut oil, or use good-quality
   vegetable oil (see page 13)
20 g/½ cup freshly chopped coriander/
   cilantro leaves and stalks
2 sweet potatoes (about 950 g/2 lb. 1 oz.),
   peeled, cubed, boiled and mashed
   (about 700 g/2 cups of mash)
1 teaspoon chaat masala powder,
   or use juice of 1 small lemon (about
   2 tablespoons)
½ teaspoon salt
coriander/cilantro yogurt (see page 65)
   and lemon wedges, to serve

CASHEW CACHUMBA CHAAT
½ cucumber, roughly peeled, fully
   deseeded and cut into 5-mm/¼-in. dice
1 small red onion, cut into 5-mm/¼-in.
   dice
freshly squeezed juice of 1 lime
2–3 tablespoons pomegranate seeds,
   or use frozen and defrosted
60 g/½ cup cashew nuts, lightly toasted
   and roughly chopped
¼ teaspoon salt
2 tablespoons freshly chopped coriander/
   cilantro and/or mint
1 teaspoon chaat masala powder,
   or use dried mango powder

baking sheet, lined with parchment

MAKES 10–12

Place the peas in a small pan of boiling water and simmer until just cooked. Leave to drain and dry slightly in a colander or sieve/strainer. Using the same warm pan, dried of any water, wilt the spinach. (If using frozen spinach, defrost fully and squeeze out all the water; for chard or kale, cook for 5–10 minutes with a splash of water until completely softened.)

In a small dry pan, toast the cumin seeds over medium–high heat until their aroma is just released. Add the gram flour and toast for another minute. Transfer to a large bowl and set aside.

To the same pan, add the ginger, chillies/chiles and a teaspoon of the oil. Cook over low–medium heat for 2–3 minutes.

Meanwhile, add the peas, cooked greens and fresh coriander/cilantro to a blender or food processor and blitz to a rough paste. (If using kale, this may require extra blending to make it smooth.)

Add the green paste to the large bowl with the cumin and gram flour, then add the mashed sweet potatoes, ginger mixture, chaat masala powder and salt. Mix really well using your hands.

Shape the mixture into 10–12 small patties, approximately 2 cm/¾ in. thick and 6.5 cm/2½ in. diameter. Arrange on the lined baking sheet and place in the fridge for 30–60 minutes to set.

Prepare the chaat salad by mixing all the ingredients together, except the fresh herbs and chaat powder. Set aside.

Place a large non-stick frying pan/skillet over medium-high heat. Add ½ tablespoon coconut oil to the pan, then place the cutlets into the pan, cooking in two batches if needed. Reduce the heat to medium and cook for 3–4 minutes on each side until golden brown. Add a little more oil to the pan if needed.

To serve, add the fresh herbs to the salad and mix well. Place a couple of cutlets on each plate (or use one big platter). Top each cutlet with a heaped tablespoon of the salad, and sprinkle the top of each portion with a generous pinch of chaat masala powder. Serve with coriander/cilantro yogurt and lemon wedges.

SWEET POTATO & BUCKWHEAT PARATHAS

This is a healthful take on one of my favourite Indian breads. Buckwheat is naturally gluten-free and a great source of fibre, protein and B vitamins. The sweet potato adds an extra comforting mouthfeel. They are the perfect foil for scooping curries, or you can use them as wraps. All the comfort of a traditional paratha, with a naturally lower glycaemic index.

Place the buckwheat flour, rice flour and tapioca starch into a large bowl. Add the ajwain seeds, salt and coriander/cilantro, and mix everything well. Add the mashed sweet potato and the hot water. Using your hands, combine the mixture until it comes together in a sticky dough. Set aside for 20–30 minutes.

Using wet hands, divide the dough into six small balls. Prepare the work surface by generously flouring with buckwheat flour. The dough is very soft and requires light handling before cooking. Using well-floured hands, carefully flatten each ball on the work surface into a small, flat round. Use your hands to neaten the outside edge, then flatten using a rolling pin to about 5 mm/¼ in. thick.

Once all the dough is rolled out and ready to cook, place a wide frying pan/skillet over high heat and add just enough oil to coat the pan. Turn the heat down to medium–low. The easiest way to transfer the dough to the pan is to slide the dough round onto a lightly floured plate from the work surface, then slide the dough into the pan (the dough tears easily until it starts to cook). Cook for 2–3 minutes on each side until just golden brown. Repeat until all the parathas are cooked, adding more oil if needed, and keeping the cooked ones warm by wrapping them in a kitchen towel.

The breads are much easier to handle once cooked and can be folded around a filling of your choice, such as the tandoori sizzling tray bake (see page 27) with a drizzle of raita, or used to scoop up your favourite curries.

300 g/2½ cups buckwheat flour,
**   plus extra for dusting**
40 g/⅓ cup rice flour
1 tablespoon tapioca starch,
**   or use cornflour/cornstarch**
1 heaped teaspoon ajwain seeds
1 teaspoon salt
large handful of freshly chopped
**   coriander/cilantro**
1 sweet potato (about 400 g/14 oz.),
**   peeled, cubed, boiled and mashed**
**   (about 350 g/1 cup of mash)**
250 ml/1 cup hot water
about 2 tablespoons culinary/
**   unflavoured coconut oil, or use**
**   good-quality vegetable oil**
**   (see page 13)**

MAKES 6

Above: Traditional paratha-making on a street-food stall in Jaisalmer, Western India.

TEMPEH MUGHLAI

300 g/10½ oz. tempeh, cut into
    2.5-cm/1-in. cubes
1 tablespoon culinary/unflavoured
    coconut oil, or use good-quality
    vegetable oil (see page 13)
2 brown onions, finely chopped
4 fat garlic cloves, finely chopped,
    or use 4 teaspoons garlic paste
1-cm/½-in. thumb of fresh ginger,
    peeled and finely chopped (about
    2 teaspoons), or use 1 heaped
    teaspoon ginger paste
2 teaspoons garam masala
1 teaspoon ground coriander
½ teaspoon ground turmeric
1 teaspoon date syrup, or use pure
    maple syrup or unrefined coconut
    sugar
½–1 teaspoon salt, to taste
freshly chopped coriander/cilantro,
    to serve

MARINADE
1 teaspoon ground coriander
1 teaspoon ground cumin
1 teaspoon ground turmeric
½ teaspoon ground cardamom
¼ teaspoon ground cinnamon
½ teaspoon chilli/chili powder
160 g/¾ cup vegan 'Greek-style' yogurt
1 tablespoon freshly squeezed lemon
    juice
½ teaspoon salt

CASHEW CREAM
120 g/1 cup cashew nuts, soaked
    in 250 ml/1 cup cold water for
    2–3 hours

baking sheet, lined with parchment

SERVES 3–4

This rich and sumptuous curry would traditionally be prepared with meat. But tempeh is a substantial protein, naturally fermented and maintaining the whole soya bean/ soybean, so packed with nutrients and less processed than tofu. These days, you can often find locally made tempeh in Asian supermarkets and health food stores. Tempeh is not widely used in India, hailing from further south of the equator in Indonesia. Use other mock meats or tofu, if you prefer.

This simplified high-protein recipe is fairly quick to put together using a food processor or blender, and I often marinate the tempeh the day before, so it becomes a 30-minute recipe. The curry can be kept in the fridge for up to 1 week and freezes well. Serve with steamed rice.

In a small dry frying pan/skillet, lightly toast all the dry marinade spices for 2–3 minutes over high heat, shaking the pan and keeping the spices moving to avoid burning them. Place the yogurt, lemon juice, salt and toasted spices into a large bowl and mix really well. Add the tempeh cubes and mix to ensure they are well coated. Cover and set aside for 1–2 hours to marinate, or overnight in the fridge.

For the cashew cream, drain and rinse the cashews, then, using a food processor or blender, blitz the cashews with 250 ml/1 cup fresh water until completely smooth. Set aside.

Preheat the oven to 210°C (400°F) Gas 6.

Lay the tempeh pieces onto the lined baking sheet, and bake in the preheated oven for 15–20 minutes until starting to brown.

Meanwhile, heat the oil in a medium–large pan, add the chopped onions and fry gently over medium heat for 10–12 minutes until translucent. Add the garlic and ginger, and cook for a further 3–4 minutes, then add the garam masala, ground coriander and turmeric. Cook the spice paste for another 2–3 minutes. Add the cashew cream and date syrup, then mix well.

Once the marinated tempeh is lightly roasted, add to the pan of creamy gravy. Mix carefully, ensuring you don't break the tempeh pieces. Add salt to taste. Bring to a simmer, then serve immediately with a sprinkle of fresh coriander/cilantro.

TANDOORI SIZZLING TRAY BAKE *with pomegranate raita*

2 brown onions, cut into 2.5-cm/1-in. pieces

1 large green (bell) pepper, cut into 2.5-cm/1-in. pieces

1 large aubergine/eggplant, cut into 3-cm/1¼-in. cubes

2 courgettes/zucchini, thickly sliced

1 sweet potato (about 400 g/14 oz.), peeled and diced into 3-cm/1¼-in. cubes

2 sticks of celery, thickly sliced at an angle

400-g/14-oz. can chickpeas/garbanzo beans, drained and rinsed

MARINADE

6 fat garlic cloves, or use 2 tablespoons garlic paste

5-cm/2-in. thumb of fresh ginger, peeled, or use 2 heaped tablespoons ginger paste

2–4 green finger chillies/chiles, or use 1 teaspoon dried chilli flakes/hot red pepper flakes or chilli/chili powder

2.5-cm/1-in. thumb of fresh turmeric, peeled, or use 1 teaspoon ground turmeric

½ teaspoon fenugreek powder (optional)

1 tablespoon paprika

1 tablespoon garam masala

1 teaspoon ground cumin

1 teaspoon salt

4–5 generous tablespoons vegan yogurt

freshly squeezed juice of ½ lemon

RAITA

200 g/1 scant cup vegan 'Greek-style' yogurt

1 pomegranate, seeds removed

¼ teaspoon ground cumin

baking sheet, lined with parchment and lightly oiled

SERVES 3–4

There's nothing quite like the aroma of roasting marinade from a tandoor to remind me of northern India. For a long time I wanted to build one in my own garden in the UK. Then I moved to Italy, and now we are lucky enough to have a wood-fired stone oven in our village, which we restored for our little community to enjoy outdoor gatherings and share food together. Of course, you don't need a wood-fired oven to make this dish. Just crank the oven up high and make sure it's at full heat before you put the tray in. If you have a pizza stone, place this on the oven shelf while the oven heats up to create the stone-baked effect.

This is a super simple recipe that can be adapted for a variety of seasonal produce, and you can add extra tofu pieces if you like. The flavoursome marinade is also a straightforward spice paste that can be used on the barbeque or for any kind of roasting. These days I get to use pomegranates from my own garden in my raita, and from re-wilded trees growing around the village. But you can use whatever tender veggies you have like cucumber, carrot, tomato or radish.

Preheat the oven to 220°C (425°F) Gas 7.

To prepare the marinade, place all the ingredients into a blender or food processor and blitz until smooth.

Place all the prepped veggies and chickpeas/garbanzo beans into a large bowl and cover with the marinade. Using your hands, mix well so everything is well coated. Set aside for at least 1 hour to marinate.

To make the raita, mix the yogurt, pomegranate seeds and ground cumin in a bowl. Set aside.

Arrange the marinated vegetables and chickpeas/garbanzo beans evenly on the prepared baking sheet. Bake in the hot oven for 25–35 minutes until the veggies are cooked and everything is slightly browned.

This dish can be served hot or cold. Try serving inside a sweet potato and buckwheat paratha (see page 23) with a generous dressing of raita, or with quinoa upma (see page 50) or steamed wholegrain basmati rice.

MUSHROOM 'KEEMA' PARATHAS

350 g/2⅔ cups wholemeal (whole-wheat) flour, plus extra for dusting (for gluten-free, use 75 g/scant ½ cup gluten-free flour or quinoa flour, plus 75 g/scant ⅔ cup rice flour plus 150 g/scant 1¼ cups gram (chickpea/garbanzo bean) flour
½ teaspoon salt
½ teaspoon baking powder
250 ml/1 cup lukewarm water (for gluten-free, use 150 ml/⅔ cup vegan milk plus 1 tablespoon vegan yogurt)
2 tablespoons olive oil
about 2 tablespoons culinary/unflavoured coconut oil, or use good-quality vegetable oil (see page 13)
coriander/cilantro yogurt (see page 65), to serve

FILLING
2 teaspoons culinary/unflavoured coconut oil, or use good-quality vegetable oil (see page 13)
1 small red onion, finely chopped
2 fat garlic cloves, finely chopped, or use 2 teaspoons garlic paste
4-cm/1½-in. thumb of fresh ginger, peeled and finely chopped, or use 2 tablespoons ginger paste
1–2 green finger chillies/chiles, finely chopped, or use dried chilli flakes/hot red pepper flakes
½ teaspoon ground turmeric
½ teaspoon cumin seeds
½ teaspoon salt
½ tablespoon garam masala
400 g/14 oz. oyster mushrooms, torn into strips, or use field mushrooms or chestnut/cremini mushrooms, cut into 6-mm/¼-in. pieces
small handful of freshly chopped coriander/cilantro (optional)

MAKES 4

We sensed a lot of familiarity with the food as we travelled around the Punjab region of India. The links between this area and the UK are strong – Punjabi is the third most commonly spoken language in the UK. Following British labour shortages during the 1950s and later post-Partition migration, the Punjabi-British influence on subcontinent food in the UK became deliciously widespread (and indeed across India and Pakistan), from simple roadside-style dals and grills to rich and buttery curries, tandoor skewers and stuffed breads.

Punjabi food reflects the richness of its agriculture, and is traditionally heavy with meat and dairy. I used to make a plant-based mock meat version of keema-stuffed bread, but mushrooms are much less processed and are rich in B6 and potassium. You can also use gluten-free flour for this recipe, if you like, but ensure you follow the ingredient adjustments.

Mix the flour(s), salt and baking powder together in a large bowl. Make a well, and add the water (or milk and yogurt if making gluten-free) and olive oil. Combine to make a soft dough, kneading for 5–6 minutes until smooth and elastic. Cover with a damp kitchen towel. Set aside in a warm place for at least 1 hour.

Prepare the filling by placing a heavy-bottomed pan over low–medium heat. Add the coconut oil, onion and garlic, and fry until the onion is softened and translucent, about 8–10 minutes.

Add the ginger, chillies/chiles, turmeric and cumin to the pan, then fry for another few minutes, before adding the salt, garam masala and mushrooms, mixing well. Cover the pan with a lid and cook for 2–3 minutes until the mushrooms start to soften. Remove the lid and cook for 3–4 minutes until fully cooked. Add the coriander/cilantro, if using, and mix well. Let cool.

Divide the dough into four balls. On a well-floured surface, use a rolling pin to flatten a ball into a 12-cm/4¾-in. round. Add one-quarter of the filling to the centre and fold the edges into the centre, making 6–7 folds around the edge. Very gently flatten the paratha again, carefully pushing any air out of the centre. Roll until you have a 12-cm/4¾-in. disc, about 1 cm/½ in. thick. Repeat with the remaining dough balls and filling.

Gently heat 1 tablespoon of the coconut oil in a large frying pan/skillet. Fry the paratha over medium–high heat for 2–3 minutes on each side until golden brown. Drain on paper towels. Repeat with the remaining parathas, adding more oil as needed. Cut each paratha into slices and serve with coriander/cilantro yogurt.

SEASONAL SABZI
Classic Pakistani vegetable curry

1–2 tablespoons culinary/unflavoured coconut oil, or use good-quality vegetable oil (see page 13)

1 teaspoon cumin seeds

2 brown onions, finely chopped

4 fat garlic cloves, finely chopped, or use 4 teaspoons garlic paste

5-cm/2-in. thumb of fresh ginger, peeled and finely chopped, or use 2 heaped tablespoons ginger paste

1–2 green chillies/chiles, sliced, to taste (optional)

½ teaspoon mustard seeds

1 teaspoon ground turmeric

1 teaspoon ground coriander

½–1 teaspoon chilli/chili powder, to taste

1 teaspoon salt

½ cauliflower, fresh or frozen, cut into bite-sized florets (optional)

½ small green or white cabbage, roughly chopped into 5-cm/2-in. pieces, or use kale

large handful of green/French beans, fresh or frozen, trimmed, or use carrot, peeled and thickly sliced

2 tomatoes, roughly chopped, or use 14–16 cherry tomatoes, halved

2 large handfuls of fresh spinach (optional)

SERVES 4

Everyone loves Manchester's 'rice n three' cafés, clustered around the old factory areas in the Northern Quarter of the city centre and located along most of the major radial roads. I know we're not the only lucky city in the UK with an abundance of these simple cafés. Mostly offering Pakistani-influenced dishes, these places are always packed at lunchtimes with office workers on plastic seating or benches around old Formica tables. There will nearly always be a seasonal vegetable sabzi on offer, a drier curry that works best with simple vegetables like cabbage, cauliflower or radish and green/French beans or carrot.

Place a large heavy-bottomed pan over medium–high heat. Add 1 tablespoon of oil and the cumin seeds, and cook until the seeds start to sizzle. Add the onions, then reduce the heat slightly and cook the onions for 10–12 minutes until translucent.

Add the garlic, ginger and chilli(es)/chile(s), if using, and cook for a further 3–4 minutes, adding a little more oil if needed. Add the mustard seeds, turmeric, ground coriander, chilli/chili powder and salt. Mix well and cook for 1–2 minutes, then add about 2–3 tablespoons water to loosen the spice paste.

Add the cauliflower, if using, and cook for 2–3 minutes. Then add the cabbage and green/French beans. Cook over high heat for 6–8 minutes, stirring often. Once the vegetables are almost tender, add the tomatoes and spinach (if using), then cook for a further 1–2 minutes until the tomatoes are just softening and the spinach has wilted. Mix everything well and then remove from the heat.

Serve the sabzi with a paratha and some raita for a light meal, or alongside some creamy super green saag tofu (see page 32), dal and rice, for a simple 'rice and three' thali at home.

Left: Himalayan sunset, Manali, Himachel Pradesh, Northern India.

CREAMY SUPER GREEN SAAG TOFU

300 g/10½ oz. firm tofu/beancurd,
    cut into 2-cm/¾-in. pieces
1–2 tablespoons good-quality oil,
    such as culinary/unflavoured coconut
    oil or avocado oil
2 brown onions, roughly chopped
3–4 fat garlic cloves, to taste, finely
    chopped, or use 3–4 teaspoons
    garlic paste
5-cm/2-in. thumb of fresh ginger,
    peeled and finely chopped, or use
    2 heaped tablespoons ginger paste
120 g/3 cups kale, or use spring greens
    or collard greens
1 heaped teaspoon ground cumin
2–3 green chillies/chiles, roughly
    chopped, or use 1 teaspoon chilli/
    chili powder
300 g/6 cups fresh spinach, or use
    350 g/2 cups frozen (you can also
    use canned, but this will have a higher
    salt content)
3 tomatoes, cored and sliced
1½ tablespoons garam masala
2 tablespoons dried methi/fenugreek
    leaves, or use large handful of fresh
60–120 ml/¼–½ cup cashew cream
    (see page 24), to taste, or use
    ready-made vegan cream
1 tablespoon freshly squeezed lemon
    juice
½–1 teaspoon salt, to taste

baking sheet, lined with parchment

SERVES 3–4

The saag paneer we all know and love in the UK firmly has its roots in North Indian, or, more specifically, Punjabi cooking. But that rich and creamy sauce with deep-fried cheese curds is definitely not the healthy option, which seems a pity given all the deliciously spiced greens.

This is a high-protein and super-healthy twist on a classic, giving all the creamy comfort notes of the original, and blending everything together to create an easy mid-week curry. I often batch-cook this sauce, as it freezes really well, then add tofu or vegetables to make a super-fast healthy dinner. Chickpeas/garbanzo beans also make a good alternative to tofu.

Preheat the oven to 180°C (350°F) Gas 4.

Arrange the tofu pieces on the lined baking sheet and bake in the preheated oven for 15 minutes until lightly crisped. Remove and set aside.

Place a heavy-bottomed pan over low heat, add the oil and the onions and cook for 12–15 minutes until the onions are softened and translucent. Add the garlic, ginger and kale and cook for a further 5 minutes.

Add the cumin and chillies/chiles, cook for 2 minutes and then add the spinach and tomatoes (if using frozen spinach, defrost first and squeeze out excess water). Combine everything well and add the garam masala and dried methi/fungreek. Bring to a simmer and cook gently for 10 minutes until everything is well softened. Using a stick blender or food processor, blend to a smooth green sauce.

Return the sauce to the pan and add the tofu pieces. Bring to a simmer and add the cream (adjust the quantity to your liking) and the lemon juice. Stir well and remove from the heat. Season with salt. Serve with sweet potato and buckwheat parathas (see page 23) and cashew cachumba chaat (see page 20).

KAJU KHUMB MAKHANE
Rajasthani-style mushrooms with cashews & lotus seeds

1½ teaspoons chilli/chili powder

1 teaspoon ground turmeric

1 teaspoon ground coriander

3 tablespoons culinary/unflavoured coconut oil, or use good-quality vegetable oil (see page 13)

1 brown onion, finely chopped

1 teaspoon nigella/kalonji seeds

1 teaspoon cumin seeds

5-cm/2-in. thumb of fresh ginger, peeled and finely chopped, or use 2 heaped tablespoons ginger paste

4–5 fat garlic cloves, to taste, finely chopped, or use 4–5 teaspoons garlic paste

1 large tomato, chopped

160 g/¾ cup Greek-style vegan yogurt

½–1 teaspoon salt, to taste

4 portobello or field mushrooms, cleaned and cut into 1-cm/½-in. thick slices

2 heaped tablespoons lotus seeds, lightly toasted

60 g/½ cup cashew nuts, lightly toasted and roughly chopped

freshly chopped coriander/cilantro, to garnish

SERVES 3–4

The magnificent state of Rajasthan is a vast land of spectacular history, ancient palaces, forts and temples. Jaipur, also known as the pink city, with its UNESCO status, is a central stop on the western tourist circuit (along with Delhi and Agra). The blue city of Jodhpur sparkles further west, set in the stark landscape of the Thar desert and the Marwar region. It is thanks to the Marwari people, who adhered to a simple vegetarian diet, that Marwari-style vegetarian restaurants (known as Marwari Bhojnalaya) spread across India and beyond.

This dish traditionally includes lotus seeds (makhana), which are rich in antioxidants and key nutrients, especially potassium, magnesium, calcium and folate, but you can easily omit these if you can't get hold of any. You can also use any mushrooms, but using griddled field mushrooms creates a meaty centrepiece. Whilst yogurt is widely used in Rajasthani cooking, it's super easy to substitute a plant-based alternative.

Place all the ground spices into a small bowl, add 4 tablespoons water and mix well.

Place a large heavy-bottomed pan over medium heat, add 2 tablespoons of the oil and the onion, and fry gently for about 7–8 minutes until softened and translucent. Now add the nigella and cumin seeds, and cook until they start to splutter. Then add the ginger and garlic. Stir well and cook gently for 2 minutes, then add the spice mixture and cook for another 2 minutes.

Add the tomato, stir well and fry the mixture for a further 5 minutes until the tomato is well cooked and the oil starts to separate out.

Remove the pan from the heat and add the yogurt, ½ teaspoon salt and 200 ml/scant 1 cup water. Bring the sauce to the boil and simmer for a few minutes to thicken. Taste and add more salt if needed.

Add the remaining 1 tablespoon oil to a ridged griddle/grill pan (or use a wide frying pan/skillet), place over high heat and arrange the mushroom slices in the pan. Fry on each side for 2 minutes until golden brown. Arrange the mushrooms on a large serving platter.

Add the lotus seeds and three-quarters of the chopped cashews to the sauce, then pour the sauce over the mushrooms. Scatter the top with the remaining chopped cashews and some coriander/cilantro. Serve with steamed wholegrain basmati or cauliflower rice for a lower carb option.

TURMERIC COCONUT BARFI

We all need a little treat from time to time. Unfortunately refined sugar, the go-to treat for most of us, is one of the most inflammatory foods we can eat, especially when eaten in excess. The scientific facts about the impacts of high sugar consumption are even played out in the form of taxation these days. Research suggests it is more addictive than cocaine and may even contribute to the development of Alzheimer's. The key to a healthy sweet treat is to ensure it is also packed with lots of other nutrients, so it doesn't just form empty calories. Healthy fats and proteins also play an important role in preventing insulin spikes. Indian barfi is usually packed with sugar and unhealthy fats from condensed milk. Vegan condensed milk also has sugar as its primary ingredient, so never be fooled into equating the term 'plant-based' with healthy. This adapted recipe uses dates with unsweetened oat milk to create a rich, sweet cream instead.

15 plump pitted dates
4 tablespoons unsweetened oat or soya/soy milk
4-cm/1½-in. thumb of fresh turmeric, peeled, or use 1 teaspoon of ground turmeric
1 tablespoon extra-virgin coconut oil
45 g/scant ½ cup blanched ground almonds
70 g/scant 1 cup desiccated/dried unsweetened shredded coconut, plus 1 tablespoon for sprinkling
1 scant teaspoon ground green cardamom seeds

20–25-cm/8–10-in. square baking pan, greased with extra-virgin coconut oil and base-lined with parchment

MAKES 16

Combine the dates, milk and fresh turmeric root (if using powder, add later) in a blender or food processor and blitz until you have a smooth paste.

Add the coconut oil to a small heavy-bottomed pan and place over medium–high heat. Once the oil is fully melted, add the date purée. Bring to a simmer, then reduce the heat to low and cook gently for about 5–6 minutes, being careful not to burn it.

Next, add the blanched ground almonds, keeping the heat on low, and mix well to form a soft dough. Then add the coconut and cardamom (and ground turmeric, if using). Remove from the heat, and mix or knead until everything is evenly combined.

Press the mixture into the greased and lined baking pan, and, using the back of an oiled spoon, spread the mixture evenly until it is smooth. Sprinkle the extra 1 tablespoon coconut on the top, pressing down lightly. Chill for 1 hour in the fridge.

Remove from the pan by running a knife around the edge and carefully tipping it out onto a board. Cut into diamond or square shapes, and store in an airtight container in the fridge for up to 1 week.

Mumbai to Kerala

Arriving in Mumbai marked a second phase in our journey across India. As much as we had loved our mountain and festival adventures so far, we were excited to be hitting some warmer weather. It felt a world away from the other crowded cities we had travelled through. Of course Mumbai is as dense as any city, more so in fact. But we were ready for a little taste of modernity and, dare I say, organization.

It started with our train arriving into the station barely one minute late after a 27½-hour journey. We were greeted by the iconic black and white taxis as we negotiated a trip to Colaba via a relatively laid-back tout. We found rooms at the formerly fabulous Shelley's, an iconic colonial budget guesthouse overlooking the harbour, with its bobbing white boats and hazy outlines of Butcher and Elephant islands in the distance. We took tea on the terrace, and enjoyed several days exploring the city and frequenting Parsi cafes. We appreciated the gentler harassment from touts and finding havens of peace and relative order watching cricketers play on the Oval Maidan, a large recreational park area where spitting and touting are firmly banned.

Our journeys south from here took us through Goa, Karnataka, Tamil Nadu and Kerala. We enjoyed the relative luxury of a train journey in our second class air-con sleeper, with Velcro curtains for privacy. The heat surging through open doors as the train made its first dawn stop at some steamy tropical-looking town reminded us why we chose the air con. The children were always in fine fettle on train journeys, with a ready supply of fresh pakoras, lentil dumplings and a cheeky treat of Indian pop. Being woken up to the calling 'puri, puri, pureeeee… chai di chai di chaieeeee' always guaranteed that they'd start the day smiling. They less preferred being bounced through the night on buses, once witnessing a young Indian woman being catapulted from her bed by a 3am emergency stop! We always chose our beds at the sides, not the back, after that.

We sometimes joined other travellers in a shared four-wheel drive to take on more brutal roads: the road to Hampi, for example, where World Heritage temples erupt out of the boulder-strewn landscape, but the potholed roads tested our mettle to get there, jarring our bodies into exhaustion. We warmed ourselves lazing the days away on Goa's sandy beaches, and in the spiritual warmth of Karnataka and their gloriously painted cows. I re-established my yoga and meditation practice that I'd let slip since the Himalaya. And then we were off again, from Mangalore to Mysore, Coimbatore to Pondicherry, we weaved our way to the southernmost state of Kerala. Dosas, oothapam, lentil vadas and potato bondas became the street-food staples of our diet. Punjabi food is considered some of the best food in the country, but southern Indian cooking holds a big piece of my foodie heart.

We clattered into some travel walls, of course. It would be impossible not to face quite a few during such a long stint, especially travelling with young children and bound by our Western shackles of distrust and closed-off hearts. We felt hounded in Agra and invisible in Mangalore, and there were times when the filth and decay became so overwhelming we could not accept seeing people, so often children, living in such dire circumstance. But then something would happen, it could be the smallest thing: a crinkly smile from the eyes of a burkha-clad woman in a busy market; sharing a

home-cooked tiffin lunch with another family in our shared train cabin; or stepping barefoot into a temple that feels as old as time, and feeling the vibrations of devotion and prayers fill your heart with something you can't explain. It took me nearly three months to allow myself to wholly love India, and allow it to love me back. India challenges you in ways you expect, and then some. But it also opens you up to clarity and connection, to what's around you and beyond you. And then it stays with you wherever you go, calling for you to return soon.

Clockwise from top left: Old fishing boat on the steamy Keralan backwaters; The historic Chhatrapati Shivaji Terminus UNESCO World Heritage railway station, Mumbai; Painted holy cow, Tamil Nadu; School children playing, Fort Cochin, Kerala; Iconic taxi, Mumbai.

MALAI MASALA
Roasted marinated broccoli in a creamy sauce

The Mughli brothers have built a Manchester institution in the heart of Rusholme's famous 'curry mile'. They've earned their rock-solid reputation by serving their family recipes, modern street food and delights from the tandoor. They've also stayed ahead of the vegan food game, serving more than fried snacks and dals. The brothers visited me back in 2013 during my street food days and said very complimentary things about my food, which perhaps inspired some ideas for their modern Indian street food menu in a restaurant setting. This recipe is inspired by their more recent menu (with their kind permission) – a plant-based delight all fired up from their beloved tandoor.

Place the marinade ingredients and 2–3 tablespoons cold water in a blender or food processor and blitz to a smooth, thick cream.

Place the broccoli in a large bowl, add the marinade and thickly coat the pieces in the marinade. Set aside for 1 hour.

To make the sauce, place a heavy-bottomed pan over medium heat, add the oil, cassia, cloves, cardamom and onions. Fry gently until the onions are softened and fragrant. Add the ginger and powdered spices, and fry for a further 2–3 minutes. Add the chopped tomatoes, salt, date syrup and 60 ml/¼ cup water, mixing everything well (if using tomato paste, add 350 ml/1½ cups of water to the pan). Bring to the boil, then reduce the heat to medium–low and simmer for 7–8 minutes.

Remove the pan from the heat and take out the bark. Add the sauce to a food processor or blender along with the vegan milk or cream and blitz until smooth. Set aside.

Preheat the oven to 220°C (425°F) Gas 7.

Arrange the broccoli pieces on the lined baking sheet and bake in the hot oven for 20 minutes until the broccoli is just tender and the pieces have started to lightly brown.

Heat the sauce and pour onto a large serving platter or into a wide bowl. Arrange the roasted broccoli pieces on top, then scatter with the pomegranate seeds, toasted almonds and coriander/cilantro. Serve immediately with steamed basmati rice.

1 large head of broccoli, quartered lengthways, including stem

MARINADE
2 fat garlic cloves, or use 2 teaspoons garlic paste
2.5-cm/1-in. thumb of fresh ginger, peeled, or use 1 heaped tablespoon ginger paste
60 g/½ cup cashew nuts, soaked overnight in cold water, then drained
½ teaspoon white pepper
1–2 green chillies/chiles, to taste
½ teaspoon salt

SAUCE
1 tablespoon culinary/unflavoured coconut oil, or use good-quality vegetable oil (see page 13)
1 stick of cassia bark, or use cinnamon bark or a pinch of ground cinnamon
4 cloves
seeds of 4 green cardamom pods
2 brown onions, roughly chopped
5-cm/2-in. thumb of fresh ginger, peeled, or use 2 heaped tablespoons ginger paste
1 tablespoon paprika
1 teaspoon fenugreek powder
½–1 teaspoon deggi mirch chilli/chili powder
400-g/14-oz. can peeled chopped plum tomatoes, or use 2 tablespoons tomato paste
large pinch of salt
½ tablespoon date syrup, or use pure maple syrup or unrefined coconut sugar
2–3 tablespoons oat or soya/soy milk or cream

TO SERVE
1 tablespoon fresh pomegranate seeds
small handful of flaked/sliced almonds, lightly toasted
small handful of freshly chopped coriander/cilantro

baking sheet, lined with parchment

SERVES 2 AS A MAIN, OR 4–5 AS AN ACCOMPANIMENT

TOFU BHURJI

½ teaspoon cumin seeds
½ tablespoon culinary/unflavoured coconut oil, or use good-quality vegetable oil (see page 13)
2 fat garlic cloves, finely chopped, or use 2 teaspoons garlic paste
2–3 spring onions/scallions, thinly sliced
1–2 green chillies/chiles, finely chopped
180 g/6½ oz. firm tofu/beancurd
½ teaspoon ground turmeric
¼ teaspoon red chilli/chili powder
2 tablespoons vegan yogurt
1 tomato, diced
½ red (bell) pepper, diced (optional)
¼ teaspoon black salt/kala salt, or use ½ teaspoon salt

SERVES 2–3

This classic Indian street food dish packs all the flavours into breakfast, brunch or afternoon snacking, inspired by the Parsi egg dish 'akuri'. Mumbai is the home of Parsi (Irani) cafés. These diners began to emerge during the early 19th century after Zoroastrians fled persecution in Persia. They became popular across the city communities, not least because whilst Indian society was shackled by caste systems and taboos, the Parsi cafés offered a table for everyone regardless of class, religion or ethnicity... which makes them the perfect place to sit, eat and watch the world go by.

This tofu scramble makes a tasty protein-rich vegan breakfast, and can be served wrapped up in an oatie roti (see page 46), mushroom keema paratha (see page 28) or with oothapam and masala beans (see page 43) as part of a big Indian brunch. (Recipe pictured on page 45.)

Place the cumin seeds in a dry frying pan/skillet and set over medium–high heat. Toast for 1–2 minutes, tossing gently, then add the oil, garlic and spring onions/scallions. Turn down the heat to low, and gently cook until the spring onions/scallions and garlic are softened and translucent.

Add the chilli(es)/chile(s), then crumble the tofu into the pan and add the ground turmeric, chilli/chili powder and half the yogurt. Mix well and cook over medium heat for 2 minutes.

Add the tomato and red (bell) pepper (if using) and cook on high for a further 2–3 minutes. Season with the salt and mix in the remaining yogurt. Serve immediately.

OOTHAPAM BRUNCH CAKES
Indian crumpets with mushrooms & masala beans

300 g/2 cups fine semolina, or use fine polenta/cornmeal for gluten-free
300 g/1⅓ cups vegan 'Greek-style' yogurt
1 tablespoon freshly squeezed lemon juice
1 teaspoon bicarbonate of soda/baking soda
1 teaspoon salt
½ teaspoon fenugreek powder
large pinch of asafoetida (hing) (optional)
½ tablespoon culinary/unflavoured coconut oil, or good-quality vegetable oil (see page 13)
2–3 mushrooms, sliced
pinch of mustard seeds (optional)
20–25 fresh or dried curry leaves, to taste (optional)

MASALA BEANS
½ tablespoon culinary/unflavoured coconut oil, or good-quality vegetable oil (see page 13)
1 fat garlic clove, finely chopped, or use 1 teaspoon garlic paste
1–2 green chillies/chiles, finely chopped
2 spring onions/scallions, thinly sliced and separated into white and green parts
1 teaspoon garam masala
½ teaspoon ground turmeric
400-g/14-oz. can baked beans
4–5 cherry tomatoes, quartered, or use 1 teaspoon tomato paste
large pinch of salt
freshly chopped coriander/cilantro, to serve (optional)

SERVES 4

The underrated sibling of the magnificent dosa, the fluffy oothapam is also made from fermented rice and urad dal. It is naturally gluten-free, comforting and substantial. Fermented batter is easy to make, but a little time-consuming, and it requires overnight standing time (see pages 56–59). This recipe is a quick non-fermented version using fine semolina as an alternative, the coarser middle part of durum wheat. For a gluten-free alternative I use fine polenta/cornmeal, which gives a grainier texture. It is essential to use finely ground for this recipe, whether you're using semolina or polenta/cornmeal. (Recipe pictured on page 44.)

Prepare the batter by mixing the semolina, yogurt, lemon juice, bicarbonate of soda/baking soda, salt, fenugreek powder and asafoetida (if using) in a medium bowl. Add enough water to make a thick pouring consistency. Set aside for 20–30 minutes.

Place a large non-stick frying pan/skillet over medium heat and add the coconut oil. Using a large spoon, pour the batter into small rounds on the hot pan, to make crumpet-sized cakes. Top each oothapam with a few mushroom slices, using the back of a spoon to gently press the mushrooms into the batter. Add a sprinkle of mustard seeds and curry leaves, if using. Fry gently for 3–4 minutes, then turn over and cook mushroom side-down for a further 3–4 minutes. Place the cooked oothapam on a baking tray in a warm oven, whilst you cook the remaining cakes.

For the masala beans, place a small pan over low heat and add the oil, garlic and chilli(es)/chile(s). Cook gently until the garlic is just cooked, then add the whites of the spring onions/scallions, the garam masala and turmeric. Cook for another 30 seconds, mixing well and then add the beans, tomatoes and salt. Bring to a simmer and cook for 2–3 minutes. Finally, add the spring onion/scallion greens and combine well.

To serve, place two or three oothapam cakes onto a plate and top with the masala beans and a sprinkle of fresh coriander/cilantro, if you like. Serve with tofu bhurji (see page 42) for an Indian brunching feast.

OATIE ROTI

When I moved to rural Italy, I did not expect to make a new Mancunian vegan friend in the neighbouring village. Sarah also happens to be a passionate health-conscious cook. We share many meals together whilst practising our terrible Italian. When I first stopped eating gluten (in my endeavours to heal an autoimmune disease), it was extraordinarily challenging and I felt I shifted from THAT awkward vegetarian to the difficult diner with food intolerances when trying to eat out, especially at friends' houses. Sarah, however, constantly surprises me with her culinary inquisitiveness and obsession for online cooking videos (and Italian tutorials). And so I was introduced to the healthy wonder that is an oatie roti.

The key to preparing these roti, is to ensure that your flour is well-sifted, especially if you grind your own oat flour (which is very easy to do and much more economical). It's also important to cook these roti a little more slowly than a wheat flour roti, and be mindful not to overcook them in order to achieve a soft texture.

185 g/3 cups rolled/
   old-fashioned oats
1 teaspoon salt
½ teaspoon ajwain seeds
1 teaspoon baking powder
300 ml/1¼ cups lukewarm water
1 tablespoon culinary/unflavoured
   coconut oil, or use olive oil

MAKES 6

First prepare the oat flour. Place the oats in a blender or food processor and blitz to a fine powder. Sift the oat flour into a large bowl, returning anything left in the sieve/strainer back to the blender and blitzing again. Sift the remaining flour into the bowl, discarding anything left in the sieve/strainer (or use for porridge). Set aside a couple of tablespoons of the oat flour to dust the rolling surface later.

Add the salt, ajwain seeds and baking powder to the bowl, mixing well. Make a well in the middle and pour in the water, then gradually combine to make a soft, sticky dough. Knead gently for a few minutes, then cover or wrap in clingfilm/plastic wrap and set aside for 20–30 minutes. The dough will become a little firmer.

Unwrap the dough and divide into six pieces, kneading slightly and rolling into small balls. Lightly flour the work surface and rolling pin, then roll out a ball of dough into a small round, approximately 3 mm/⅛ in. thick. Place on a plate, cover with a damp kitchen towel and repeat with the remaining dough balls.

Place a wide frying pan/skillet or tawa over medium heat and add a little oil. Cook the rotis, one at a time, for about 2–4 minutes, turning occasionally. Wrap the cooked rotis in a dry kitchen towel to keep them warm as you cook the rest. Serve immediately.

BAKED GOBI MANCHURIAN

A firm favourite on Indo-British restaurant menus, we were surprised to see this is an equally popular dish across many southern Indian city menus. This recipe is my healthier version, baked instead of fried and with less added sugar. Equally sticky, crispy and deliciously moreish!

Preheat the oven to 220°C (425°F) Gas 7.

Combine the dry batter ingredients in a large bowl and toss the cauliflower pieces in the dry mixture. Remove the pieces and set aside on a plate. Now add 5–6 tablespoons water and the soy sauce to the remaining dry mixture to make a cream-like batter that coats the back of a spoon. Add more water if needed.

Dip the cauliflower florets in the mixture, gently shake off any excess batter, then place the pieces onto the lined and oiled baking sheet. You may need to add a little more water to the batter as you go, as it will thicken whilst you are dipping the pieces. Ensure the cauliflower pieces are spaced well apart on the baking sheet so they cook evenly and don't stick together. Spray with a little cooking oil spray or drizzle with a few teaspoons of oil if you prefer a crispier texture.

Bake in the hot oven for 20–25 minutes until the cauliflower pieces are crisp and browning. (The florets can be reheated to crisp up again, so can be prepared earlier and set aside.)

Meanwhile, for the sauce, place a wok or deep frying pan/skillet over medium–high heat and add the oil. Add the chillies/chiles, ginger and celery, and stir-fry for 3–4 minutes, then add the garlic, green (bell) pepper and white parts of the spring onions/scallions. Cook for a further 2–3 minutes.

Add all the remaining ingredients (except for the spring onion/scallion greens) to the pan along with 625 ml/2½ cups water. Mix well and bring to a simmer, cooking gently over low heat for about 5–8 minutes until the flour is cooked through and the sauce is thickened and glossy.

To serve, arrange the baked cauliflower pieces on a serving platter and pour over the sauce, ensuring all the pieces are well coated. Scatter with the sliced spring onion/scallion greens and serve immediately.

1 cauliflower, cut into florets
cooking oil spray, or use good-quality
  vegetable oil (see page 13)

BATTER
65 g/scant ½ cup plain/all-purpose
  flour, or use gluten-free or gram
  (chickpea/garbanzo bean) flour
65 g/scant ½ cup cornflour/cornstarch,
  or use potato flour
1 teaspoon deghi mirch chilli/chili
  powder, or use kashmiri or any mild
  chilli/chili powder
¼ teaspoon ground turmeric
¼ teaspoon black pepper
½ teaspoon salt
1 tablespoon soy sauce

SAUCE
1 teaspoon culinary/unflavoured
  coconut oil, or use good-quality
  vegetable oil (see page 13)
2 green or red chillies/chiles, finely
  chopped
5-cm/2-in. thumb of fresh ginger,
  peeled and finely chopped, or use
  2 heaped tablespoons ginger paste
1 small stick of celery, finely diced
6 fat garlic cloves, finely chopped,
  or use 2 tablespoons garlic paste
½ green (bell) pepper, finely diced
2 spring onions/scallions, sliced and
  separated into white and green parts
1½ tablespoons cornflour/cornstarch,
  made into a paste with
  4–5 tablespoons cold water
2 tablespoons tomato ketchup, or use
  1 tablespoon tomato purée/paste
  plus 1 teaspoon date syrup
1 tablespoon sambol olek, or use
  unsweetened chilli/chili sauce
  or 1 teaspoon chilli/chili paste
1 teaspoon rice vinegar
1 tablespoon soy sauce
½–1 teaspoon salt, to taste
¼ teaspoon ground black pepper

*baking sheet, lined with parchment
and lightly oiled*

SERVES 4

QUINOA UPMA

340 g/2 cups quinoa, try using mixed
  varieties of red and white for colour
1 whole dried red chilli/chile
1 tablespoon good-quality oil for frying
  (see page 13), such as avocado oil or
  culinary/unflavoured coconut oil
20 fresh or dried curry leaves
1 teaspoon mustard seeds
1 brown onion, finely chopped
1-cm/½-in. thumb of fresh ginger,
  peeled and finely chopped (about
  2 teaspoons), or use 1 heaped
  teaspoon ginger paste
¼ teaspoon chilli/chili powder
1 green chilli/chile, thinly sliced
½ teaspoon date syrup, or use pure
  maple syrup or unrefined coconut
  sugar
freshly squeezed juice of ½ lemon
½–1 teaspoon salt, to taste
8–10 cherry tomatoes, halved
handful of freshly torn basil (Thai is
  preferable, but Italian or Greek basil,
  or fresh coriander/cilantro, also work
  well), to serve

SERVES 4

In my first book, Vegan Street Food, I wrote a section about how to make tofu taste good. I sometimes feel like quinoa also needs a cheerleader like this (I'd add chia to this list, too). Quinoa is far less flavourful than the beautifully diverse varieties of rice that can be found across Asia. But it is incredibly healthful and packed with protein and all the amino acids we need. Quinoa just needs a helping hand. Perhaps it should have a word with kale's marketing manager!

Upma is a traditional breakfast from South India, made from toasted semolina or rice made into a thick, savoury porridge with various vegetables and spices. The flavours are fired up by the sizzling tarka-like fry with mustard seeds, curry leaves, fresh chilli/chile and ginger. This quinoa version is one of my favourite rice alternatives, or it can be served as part of an Indian brunch with tofu bhurji (see page 42).

Prepare the quinoa by rinsing well in a sieve/strainer, then add to a small pan and cover with water. Bring to the boil, then reduce the heat and simmer for 10–12 minutes until the quinoa is cooked. Drain in a sieve/strainer and set aside.

Place a wok or deep frying pan/skillet over high heat and tear the dried chilli/chile into large pieces straight into the pan (that way you won't lose any seeds). Toast the dried chilli/chile in the hot pan until just starting to colour, then add the oil, curry leaves and mustard seeds. As the seeds start to pop, add the onion and sauté over low heat for 10–12 minutes until the onion is translucent and soft. Add the ginger, chilli/chili powder and green chilli/chile, mixing well, and continue to sauté for 1–2 minutes.

Add the cooked quinoa to the pan, along with the date syrup, lemon juice and ½ teaspoon salt. Combine everything well and add more salt to taste, if needed. Return the mixture to a medium–high heat and add the tomatoes. Cook for 1–2 minutes, then remove from the heat and add the torn basil. Mix well and serve immediately.

BAGHARE BAINGAN
Spicy, sweet & sour aubergines/ eggplants with black chickpeas

When we travelled across Southern India, monsoon rain had damaged the railway lines and we were faced with some of our first overnight public bus journeys in India. We'd taken many short trips during our previous four months, and whilst these were sometimes slightly hair-raising journeys, travelling with young children opened the door to meeting so many local people, especially other families. Sharing food and playing games, whilst chatting about what my 'very good father' does for a living. The twins were often the star attraction on the bus (or railway platform). Unless someone fell off the roof. Although officials seemed to be trying to put a stop to that.

This is a special curry from Hyderabad, the capital of the southern Indian state of Telangana. Where once upon a time money was made from diamond-trading, the city has now emerged as a centre for the tech industry. Fewer travellers come through Hyderabad, as the well-travelled southern route for overlanders tends to follow the east or west coasts, then crosses the southern states of Karnataka, Andhra Pradesh and Tamil Nadu. Hyderabadi food has a princely history with Mughal, Arabic and Turkish influences, and many of their banquet dishes can be found across menus in more wealthy Indian cities, such as the much-celebrated goat biryani.

This recipe celebrates the flavours of Hyderabadi food with a luxurious plant-based dinner, with traditional deep sour notes and umami-rich flavours. I've adapted the traditional recipe to make the process a little easier with some additional elements to complement the soft and creamy aubergine/eggplant. The black chickpeas – kala channa – add more protein and a nutty texture, but you could easily use standard chickpeas/garbanzo beans or add any vegetable you prefer to the gravy at the end. It looks like a long list of ingredients, but is surprisingly easy to make with a stick blender, food processor or blender.

Left: The steam trains of the Nilgiri Blue Mountain Railway, Tamil Nadu, Southern India.

4–5 small aubergines/eggplants,
   or use 8 baby aubergines/eggplants
   or 12 of the long, thin variety
½ tablespoon culinary/unflavoured
   coconut oil, or use good-quality
   vegetable oil (see page 13)
1 small brown onion, finely chopped
2 young courgettes/zucchini, thickly
   sliced, or use other tender vegetables
3 tablespoons tamarind pulp, or use
   1½ teaspoons tamarind concentrate
   plus 2 tablespoons water
400-g/14-oz can black chickpeas/
   kala channa, drained and rinsed
salt, to taste

PASTE
2 tablespoons unsalted peanuts,
   unskinned or skinned
2 tablespoons desiccated/dried
   unsweetened shredded coconut
2 teaspoons sesame seeds
1 teaspoon cumin seeds
1 tablespoon molasses, or use date
   syrup
small handful of fresh coriander/
   cilantro, including stems
1 teaspoon salt
1 teaspoon chilli/chili powder
1 teaspoon ground turmeric
5-cm/2-in. thumb of fresh ginger,
   peeled, or use 2 heaped tablespoons
   ginger paste
3 fat garlic cloves, or use 1 tablespoon
   garlic paste
1 teaspoon garam masala

TO SERVE
freshly chopped coriander/cilantro
toasted peanuts, roughly chopped
   (optional)
lemon wedges (optional)

SERVES 4

Preheat the oven to 180°C (350°F) Gas 4.

Start by making the paste. Place a wok or large deep frying pan/skillet over high heat for 1 minute, then add the peanuts and toast for 3–4 minutes, shaking the pan to avoid any burning. Add the coconut, sesame and cumin seeds, gently tossing the pan to mix and toast all the ingredients until the aromas are released. Remove from the heat and add to a food processor or blender (or into a jug/pitcher and use a stick blender).

Add the remaining spice paste ingredients to the food processor or blender along with 250 ml/1 cup water. Blitz until smooth, adding more water as needed.

To prepare the aubergines/eggplants, cut two slits lengthways to create quarters, leaving the top stem intact so that the aubergine/eggplant remains whole. If using long aubergines/eggplants that are quite thin, just slice once down the centre, keeping the stem intact. Using your hands, cover the aubergines/eggplants in the paste, pushing it inside so each quarter is well smothered. Arrange in a baking dish. Smother the remaining paste over the top and bake in the preheated oven for about 40 minutes until the aubergines/eggplants are just tender and the spice paste is well cooked.

Meanwhile, heat the oil in the same wok or frying pan/skillet, add the onion and fry gently over low–medium heat until translucent and soft. Add the courgettes/zucchini, tamarind, black chickpeas/kala channa and 300 ml/1¼ cups water and mix well. Bring to a simmer.

Transfer the cooked aubergines/eggplants back into the wok, scraping all the spice paste into the pan, too. Mix well, but be careful not to break the aubergines/eggplants. Bring the pan back to a simmer and cook for 20–30 minutes until the aubergines/eggplants are well softened. Add a little more water if needed to loosen, but not too much, as this is quite a dry curry with a thick nutty gravy. Season with salt to taste.

Scatter with fresh coriander/cilantro and toasted peanuts, if using, and serve with lemon wedges on the side, if you like. This rich flavourful dish works well with cauliflower 'rice', to ramp up the veggies and keep the carbohydrates low, or steamed basmati, if you prefer.

SIMPLE KERALAN BOATMAN'S CURRY
with roasted cauliflower, turmeric & coconut

1 cauliflower, cut into large 5–7.5-cm/2–3-in. florets
1 tablespoon culinary/unflavoured coconut oil, or use good-quality vegetable oil (see page 13)
5 small shallots, halved
3 tablespoons tamarind pulp, or use 1½ teaspoons tamarind concentrate plus 2 tablespoons water
1 teaspoon salt
2–4 green chillies/chiles, halved lengthways
freshly chopped coriander/cilantro, to garnish

SPICE PASTE
4–6 dried red chillies/chiles, to taste
3 tablespoons desiccated/dried unsweetened shredded coconut, or use 1½ tablespoons creamed coconut (hard block type)
½ teaspoon chilli/chili powder
3 tablespoons ground coriander
1 tablespoon paprika
1 teaspoon ground turmeric
2.5-cm/1-in. thumb of fresh ginger, peeled, or use 1 heaped tablespoon ginger paste

baking sheet, lightly oiled

SERVES 3–4

Kerala is a three-showers-a-day kind of place. The intense humidity builds through the day, often ending with a heavy rain storm that refreshes the atmosphere like natural air conditioning. We had been staying in Fort Cochin for a few days, a pretty little town where we had a lovely room overlooking terracotta tiled houses and listening to the sounds of hymn practice from the local school. We got up at dawn to take a boat trip floating down the Keralan backwaters. Our tiny boat glided silently through narrow and overgrown waterways, whilst we spotted snakes, kingfishers, woodpeckers, fishing cormorants and wildflowers. In the evenings, we watched the fishermen hauling in their catches at sunset, where it takes four or five of them to raise and lower the huge Chinese fishing nets from the water.

Fish and seafood are a central part of cooking here. Boatman's curry is usually made with seafood in a spicy and sour, but lightly creamy broth. This simple recipe is completely adaptable for delicious vegetables and makes a great mid-week dish that can be on the table in 30 minutes.

For the spice paste, soak the chillies/chiles and desiccated/dried unsweetened shredded coconut, if using, in boiling water for 15 minutes.

Meanwhile, preheat the oven to 190°C (375°F) Gas 5.

Arrange the cauliflower pieces on the lightly oiled baking sheet. Roast in the preheated oven for 10–12 minutes until starting to brown at the edges.

Drain the soaked chillies/chiles and desiccated/dried unsweetened shredded coconut and place them into a blender or food processor along with 200 ml/scant 1 cup water and all the other spice paste ingredients. Blitz to a smooth paste.

Place a large heavy-bottomed pan over medium heat and add the coconut oil. Place the shallots in the pan, flat-side down, and fry for 2–3 minutes until starting to soften and brown.

Add the spice paste and bring to a simmer. Cook gently over low–medium heat for a few more minutes. Add the tamarind, salt, green chillies/chiles and cauliflower pieces, then bring back to a simmer for 1–2 minutes, adding a splash of water if needed.

Garnish with chopped coriander/cilantro and serve warm with steamed brown basmati rice or quinoa upma (see page 50).

GREEN SPINACH DOSA *with seasonal mor sambhar*

We have certainly learned that everywhere can appear horrible when you arrive in the dark, travel-weary and sleep-deprived from the overnight train, especially when it also happens to be pouring with monsoonal rain. In this hyper-tired state, we fail to immediately notice the smeared dirty walls and filth-caked floor in our new room. At times like this, a bed with a clean sheet looks like the shining sun and distracts you from paying attention. And that's how we ended up booking into what must have been one of the filthiest guesthouses in Trivandrum. Considering the city is said to be one of the jewels of Kerala, it wasn't the best start. But we were here with purpose, as we tried to arrange a short flight into Sri Lanka.

We had faced a lot of challenges as a family travelling overland around southern India, which was a far cry from the spacious Himalaya or laid-back west-coast beach life. The children found the journeys harder (as we all did) and travel exhaustion and homesickness had been setting in. It's not uncommon to hit a wall like this during long-term travel, and we all felt it to some degree. We were excited to be moving on to another country, but there is a toll of reality when travelling in India (unless you hide away in upmarket hotels and resorts, but that's not what we were here to experience). So after a few days taking in some of the well-touristed rugged coastline, and some kathakali performances (a classical Indian musical play with elaborate colourful masks and costumes that slightly alarmed the children) we were ready to move on. After more than 5 months of overland travel, we organised flights for the following day and went out for our last dinner in India. The children chose, and, of course, it had to be dosa.

Our love of dosa has not faded. Fermented dosa batter is not that difficult to make, it's simply a little time-consuming with soaking and blending. But once you've made the batter once or twice, you'll find it an easy recipe to prepare in advance. This recipe incorporates extra greens in the dosa and the sambhar. This dal accompaniment is slightly easier to prepare than traditional tamarind sambhar and is also delicious served with appam (rice and coconut hoppers, recipe in Vegan Street Food). You can swap the okra for other seasonal veggies.

Left: Vizhinjam Lighthouse and Kovalam Beach, Trivandrum, Kerala, Southern India.

300 g/1¾ cups basmati rice,
    soaked overnight in cold water
100 g/½ cup urad dal, soaked
    overnight in cold water
½ teaspoon ground fenugreek
1 teaspoon salt
150 g/3 cups fresh spinach, or use
    175 g/1 cup frozen spinach (you can
    also use canned, but this will have
    a higher salt content)
good-quality vegetable oil
    (see page 13), for frying

FILLING

½ tablespoon culinary/unflavoured
    coconut oil, or use good-quality
    vegetable oil (see page 13)
1 teaspoon mustard seeds
1 dried red chilli/chile, crumbled
10 fresh or dried curry leaves
1 small brown onion, finely chopped
1 green chilli/chile, finely chopped
    (optional)
2.5-cm/1-in. thumb of fresh ginger,
    peeled, or use 1 heaped tablespoon
    ginger paste
¼ teaspoon chilli/chili powder
¼ teaspoon ground turmeric
1 sweet potato (about 400 g/14 oz.),
    peeled, cubed, boiled and mashed
    (about 350 g/1 cup of mash)
30g/¼ cup peas, fresh or frozen
1 tablespoon cashew nuts, broken
    into pieces and toasted (optional)
½ teaspoon salt

MOR SAMBHAR

60 g/⅓ cup red lentils, soaked
    overnight in cold water
1 teaspoon good-quality vegetable
    oil (see page 13)
15 okra fingers, washed and air-dried
    on paper towels, trimmed and cut
    into 2.5-cm/1-in. pieces
2 teaspoons coriander seeds
3–5 dried red chillies/chiles, to taste
½ teaspoon fenugreek/methi seeds
10–12 fresh or dried curry leaves

1 teaspoon sesame oil, or use good-
    quality vegetable oil (see page 13)
¼ teaspoon mustard seeds
¼ teaspoon asafoetida (hing) (optional)
1 heaped teaspoon garam masala
160 g/¾ cup vegan 'Greek-style' yogurt
large pinch of salt

MAKES 8–10

Drain the rice and dal, reserving the soaking water. Place
the drained rice and dal into a food processor or blender, add
250ml/1 cup of the soaking water, the fenugreek and salt, then
blitz until smooth, adding an extra 60 ml/¼ cup soaking water if
needed. Pour the mixture into a large bowl, cover with clingfilm/
plastic wrap and leave in a warm place overnight to ferment.
The batter will keep for 2–3 weeks in the fridge, or can be frozen.

The next day, place the spinach into a pan with a lid and set over
medium heat until just wilted (if using frozen spinach, defrost
and squeeze out the excess water). Place the spinach in a food
processor or blender along with about 250 ml/1 cup of the
batter mixture. Blitz until smooth. Now add the green batter
mixture back into the bowl with the rest of the batter and mix
well, adding a little more water to make a pouring consistency.

To prepare the filling, place a large frying pan/skillet over medium
heat and add the oil and mustard seeds. Cook for 1–2 minutes
until the seeds start to splutter, then add the dried chilli/chile
and curry leaves. Fry for another minute, then add the onion,
green chillie/chile (if using) and ginger, and cook for a further
5–6 minutes over low–medium heat.

Add the chilli/chili powder and ground turmeric to the pan and
cook for another minute, then add the sweet potato, peas and
cashews (if using), and mix well. Add the salt, and set aside,
either off the heat or over very low heat until ready to use.

To make the sambhar, drain and rinse the soaked lentils, then
add them to a small pan and cover with water. Bring to the boil
and simmer over high heat for 15–20 minutes until just cooked
(unsoaked lentils will take a little longer to cook). Drain the lentils,
rinse and set aside.

In a small frying pan/skillet, heat the oil over medium–high heat,
then add the okra pieces. Fry the okra for 5–6 minutes until just
browning, then transfer onto some paper towels and set aside.

In a small clean pan, dry toast the coriander seeds, dried chillies/chiles, fenugreek/methi seeds and curry leaves until just aromatic. Add the sesame oil to the pan, then add the mustard seeds and fry until they start spluttering. Now add the asafoetida, if using, garam masala and 125 ml/½ cup water. Add the lentils and bring to a simmer, then cook for 5 minutes until the lentils are completely softened. Add the okra, yogurt and another 125 ml/½ cup water. Bring back to a simmer, season to taste with salt, then remove from the heat and set aside until ready to serve.

To cook the dosa, place a large flat non-stick frying pan/skillet over medium–high heat (wide crêpe pans are perfect for this). Add a little oil, then, using a ladle, add about 200 ml/scant 1 cup batter to the centre of the pan. Using the back of the ladle and making small circular motions, smooth the batter out to the edges of the pan. If making smaller dosa, you can simply tip the pan to coat the batter across the bottom. Add a little more oil to the edges to prevent sticking. Cook over medium heat for 2–3 minutes, then add 2–3 tablespoons of filling to the centre. Fold the pancake over the filling on three sides to make a triangular shape, gently pressing the filling down slightly. Cook for another 30 seconds on each side. Repeat with the remaining batter and filling.

Serve immediately with the sambhar, and some hot chilli sambol if you like.

Above: Cruising the steamy Keralan backwaters from Alleppey, gliding past waterside villages, paddy fields, coconut groves, temples and toddy shops. Kerala, southern India.

Sri Lanka

If you've read *Vegan Street Food*, you'll know that we got married in Sri Lanka (or at least I think we did – both the ceremony and certificate are in Sinhalese, so I may have adopted him!). We spent a month in Sri Lanka during our first year away, and returned a few years later to get married. We stayed in more upmarket hotels and guesthouses during our second trip, and discovered that not all hotel buffets are where food goes to die. Bowls upon bowls of so many vegetable combinations, and unexpected mock meat offerings like young jackfruit and chunky textured vegetable protein (TVP) curries. Fermented rice hoppers (*Vegan Street Food*), nutty red rice and spicy sambols complemented the subtly varied curries and dals.

We knew from our previous trip that arranging a driver and car is the easiest way to get around, and that's how we met Prasana. Most of our trip plans this time had centred around trying to reach Nepal in good weather, so we hadn't really considered what the weather would be like in the south of the Indian subcontinent. The rainy season in the south and west of Sri Lanka begins around April, and we soon found ourselves navigating treacherous roads and muddy hikes. There were times when even Prasana looked a little concerned. Rain had stopped the railway so we made the right decision.

We climbed up Horton Plains to World's End, through cloud forests and torrential downpours. On a fine day, World's End sheer cliff sits in the centre of the south and offers views across the southern plains and coasts. Because it's a cloud forest, if you reach the summit from mid-morning onwards (or in the rainy season), the only thing you'll see is a wall of white cloud. Rainy season is also durian season. So the pungent waft of this indecipherable fruit was everywhere it seemed. Prasana tried to pretend he hadn't been eating it in the car.

There are benefits to travel during the rainy season. The sounds of the jungle crank up to stadium concert levels. Rafting becomes a whole lot more fun, as long as you choose a reputable operator who knows the rivers and flood risk areas. And whilst the seas are a little rougher, which might seem at odds with the best snorkelling, the plankton-rich water brings some of the bigger fish out to play including turtles and the ethereal manta rays. Feeling slightly spooked by the soupy water, I had been contemplating getting out, when the shadowy wings glided beneath me, and distracted me from thinking about the other big fish with teeth. Swimming with mantas was probably the best wedding present we received. The stuff that bucket lists are made of!

Clockwise from top left: Sri Lankan hill country, Ella, Central Province; Fruit seller, Galle, Southern Province; Street-food rickshaw, Colombo; Surfy beach, Kirinda, Yala, Southern Province; Buddhist stupa at Dambulla Cave Temple Complex, Matale District, Central Province.

KANDY CURRY *with potatoes, bottle gourd & cashews*

60 g/½ cup cashew nuts,
    soaked for 1 hour and drained
250 g/9 oz. potatoes, peeled and
    cut into 2-cm/¾-in. cubes
2 teaspoons extra-virgin coconut oil,
    plus extra if needed
10 fresh or dried curry leaves
5-cm/2-in. piece of pandan leaf, or
    use 1–2 drops pure vanilla extract
    (optional)
5-cm/2-in. cinnamon stick or piece
    of cassia bark
seeds of 3 green cardamom pods
1 brown onion, finely diced
2 fat garlic cloves, thinly sliced
2–3 green chillies/chiles, to taste
1 teaspoon ground turmeric
1 teaspoon mustard seeds
350 ml/1½ cups coconut milk
300 g/10½ oz. bottle gourd (local
    names are watakolu or lauki), peeled
    and cut into 2-cm/¾-in. cubes, or use
    courgettes/zucchini, but no need to
    peel them
½–1 teaspoon salt, to taste

SERVES 4–5

Sri Lankan potato curry, ala kiri hodi, is a lunchtime staple across the island. It's super easy to prepare and can be eaten simply with rice, or as it often appeared, accompanying several other dishes in a Sri Lankan-style thali. Gourd is also a very popular vegetable in Sri Lankan cooking, and bottle gourd (watakolu) is one of the most delicious, as well as being a powerhouse of essential nutrients. The added cashews give a nice crunchy texture (and extra protein) alongside the soft vegetables, but you can omit them if you prefer to make a more traditional curry.

Preheat the oven to 160°C (325°F) Gas 3.

Place the cashew nuts on a baking sheet and toast them in the preheated oven for 10–15 minutes until just starting to brown. Set aside. (To save time, you can prepare the toasted cashews in advance and store them in a clean air-tight jar until needed.)

Place a small pan of boiling water over high heat and bring to the boil. Add the potatoes, reduce the heat to a simmer, then cook for 5–7 minutes until the potatoes start to soften, taking care not to overcook. Drain in a colander and set aside.

Place a large heavy-bottomed pan over medium–high heat and add the coconut oil. Add the curry leaves, pandan leaf (if using), cinnamon, cardamom seeds and onion. Gently stir-fry for 5–6 minutes until the onion starts to soften and the aromas are released.

Next add the garlic, chillies/chiles and ground turmeric. Mix well and cook for a further 3–4 minutes over medium heat until the onion and garlic start to brown. Add a little more oil if needed. Add the mustard seeds, and cook until they start to splutter.

Add the coconut milk and bring the pan back to a low simmer, cooking gently for a further 5–6 minutes, adding a few tablespoons of water as needed so the gravy isn't too thick. Now add the potato and gourd pieces, and mix well. Bring to a simmer and cook for about 10 minutes until all the vegetables are just soft, but not falling apart.

Season with salt to taste and add the toasted cashew nuts. Serve warm with steamed rice.

ULUNDU VADAI
Baked lentil dumplings

200 g/1 cup urad dal, skinned (white), soaked overnight in hot water
1 tablespoon basmati rice, soaked overnight in cold water
2 green chillies/chiles
1 teaspoon salt
½ teaspoon white pepper
small handful of freshly chopped coriander/cilantro
½ teaspoon baking powder
½ teaspoon cumin seeds
1-cm/½-in. thumb of fresh ginger, peeled and finely chopped (about 2 teaspoons), or use 1 heaped teaspoon ginger paste
6–7 fresh or dried curry leaves, roughly chopped or crumbled (optional)
culinary/unflavoured coconut oil, or use good-quality vegetable oil (see page 13), for brushing

CORIANDER/CILANTRO YOGURT
6–8 tablespoons coconut yogurt
small handful of freshly chopped coriander/cilantro

TO SERVE
carrot, radish and coconut salad (see page 66)
lime and date chutney (see page 66)
chaat powder (optional)

baking sheet, lightly oiled

MAKES 8

This classic street food snack is popular throughout Sri Lanka and southern India (vada). Most often served with a bowl of sambar dal or with chaat-spiced yogurt and chutneys (dahi vada), and always deep-fried. I've adapted this version into a healthier recipe, by baking the Sri Lankan-style vadai and serving alongside an easy-to-make coriander/cilantro yogurt and lime and date chutney (see page 66). Or try it with mor sambhar (see page 58).

Rinse and drain the soaked urad dal and rice in a colander, then add them to a blender or food processor with the chillies/chiles, salt and pepper. Blitz until the batter is almost smooth. Do not add water as the batter should be firm (although it will be wet and sticky). Turn out into a bowl, add the chopped coriander/cilantro, baking powder, cumin seeds, ginger and curry leaves (if using), and mix well by lightly kneading.

Using oiled hands, divide the mixture into eight balls. Use your thumb to make a hole in the centre of each ball, and make a small doughnut shape. Arrange on the oiled baking sheet and leave to rest for 20 minutes.

Meanwhile, preheat the oven to 210°C (400°F) Gas 6.

Bake the dumplings in the preheated oven for 15 minutes, then turn over, brush with a little oil and bake for another 15 minutes until golden.

To make the yogurt dressing, mix together the yogurt and freshly chopped coriander/cilantro.

Arrange the warm dumplings on a plate. I like to serve them on a bed of Sri Lankan carrot, radish and coconut salad. Dollop the yogurt on top and add a drizzle of lime and date chutney. Sprinkle with chaat powder, if you like.

CARROT, RADISH & COCONUT SALAD

Raw food is an integral part of a healthy diet, and carrots appear to be one of the most ubiquitous vegetables on the planet. This is traditionally made with fresh coconut, but coarse desiccated/dried unsweetened shredded coconut makes a good substitute. Recipe pictured opposite.

2 heaped tablespoons desiccated/dried unsweetened shredded coconut
4 carrots, peeled and grated
7.5–10-cm/3–4-in. mooli/daikon radish, peeled and grated
1 large tomato, cored and cut into 6-mm/¼-in. cubes
1 small–medium red onion, finely chopped
2–3 green finger chillies/chiles, to taste, finely chopped
freshly squeezed juice of 1 lime
¼ teaspoon ground black pepper
large pinch of salt

SERVES 4–5 AS A SIDE DISH

Soak the desiccated/dried unsweetened shredded coconut in boiling water for 20–30 minutes until softened. Drain well in a sieve/strainer, squeezing out any excess water.

Place the coconut in a large bowl along with all the other ingredients, mixing everything well. Serve immediately.

LIME & DATE CHUTNEY

Chutneys and sambols are an essential part of a Sri Lankan meal. And this one is relatively simple to prepare. This delicious and popular condiment is a great classic to add to the Vegan Street Food *chutney collection. Recipe pictured on page 72.*

10–15 dried red chillies/chiles, to taste, crumbled
½ tablespoon mustard seeds
10 fat garlic cloves
4-cm/1½-in. thumb of fresh ginger, peeled, or use 2 tablespoons ginger paste
275 g/1½ cups coconut sugar, or use unrefined brown sugar
250 g/1½ cups plump whole dates, pitted and roughly chopped
4 preserved limes, cut into eighths, then thinly sliced, or use pickled lime halves
200 ml/scant 1 cup rice vinegar
70 g/½ cup sultanas/golden raisins

MAKES 500–600 ML/2–2½ CUPS

Place the chillies/chiles and mustard seeds in boiling water and leave to soak for an hour. Place in a blender or food processor with the garlic and ginger, and blitz to a paste.

Place a heavy-bottomed pan over medium–high heat. Add the blended ingredients to the pan, along with the coconut sugar. Bring to the boil, then reduce the heat and simmer over low heat for 5 minutes until the sugar is dissolved.

Add the dates, limes, vinegar and sultanas/golden raisins. Bring back to the boil, then reduce the heat to low and simmer for 15–20 minutes, or longer if it needs reducing further (the mixture should be fairly thick and sticky).

Store in a sterilized jar in the fridge for up to 8 weeks.

PUMPKIN AMBUL THIYAL
Dry-roasted sour pumpkin curry

500 g/1 lb. 2 oz. pumpkin, peeled
   and cut into 5-cm/2-in. cubes

SPICE PASTE
2 tablespoons tamarind pulp,
   or use 1 teaspoon concentrate
   plus 1½ tablespoons water
3 tablespoons black pepper
2.5-cm/1-in. thumb of fresh ginger,
   peeled, or use 1 heaped tablespoon
   ginger paste
4 fat garlic cloves, or use 4 teaspoons
   garlic paste
seeds of 3 cardamom pods
5–6 fresh or dried curry leaves
3 cloves
5-cm/2-in. piece of pandan leaf,
   or use 1–2 drops pure vanilla extract
   (optional)
1 teaspoon chilli/chili powder
¼ teaspoon ground turmeric
½–1 teaspoon salt, to taste

TO SERVE
coriander/cilantro yogurt (see page 65)
lime and date chutney (see page 66)

SERVES 4

Traditionally, ambul thiyal (meaning burnt curry) is a sour fish curry from the south, used as a method of preserving fish. This vegan version uses seasonal pumpkin, and substitutes the Sri Lankan goraka, a small sour fruit sometimes called fish tamarind, with the more widely available tamarind paste. This simplified recipe takes less than 30 minutes to prepare.

This seasonal curry can also be made using any kind of squash or even banana flower or tofu. It's a dry-style curry, best served alongside something saucy like garlic curry (see page 70) and steamed rice, with coriander/cilantro yogurt (see page 65) and lime and date chutney (see page 66).

To prepare the spice paste, blitz together all the ingredients to make a smooth paste.

Place the pumpkin pieces in a bowl and add the paste. Using your hands, mix well to ensure all the pieces are well coated. Leave to marinate for 15–20 minutes.

Lay a piece of parchment, cut to size, in the bottom of a heavy-bottomed pan with a lid. Arrange the pumpkin pieces in the pan. Add 1–2 tablespoons water to the bowl and mix it into the remaining marinade, then pour it over the pumpkin pieces.

Place the pan over low heat, cover with a lid and simmer gently over very low heat for 15–20 minutes until all the liquid evaporates. Cook for a further few minutes until the pieces just start to brown on the bottom, then remove from the heat.

Serve with coriander/cilantro yogurt, lime and date chutney and steamed brown basmati rice or cauliflower rice for lower carbohydrates.

GARLIC CURRY

A unique Sri Lankan curry rarely seen outside of the country, this garlic curry is actually a staple side dish in many households. The pungent garlic flavours are tempered through the cooking process until the cloves are soft and sweet. We enjoyed this dish as part of our wedding banquet, and were taken aback by how moreish this simple curry of simmered sticky garlic was, as we scraped the bowl clean. We had spent the morning laying out our wedding clothes and relaxing in the garden overlooking the river valley, and watching the bathing water buffalo. The peacefulness occasionally punctuated by shouts from the kitchen and a scurrying young kitchen boy running to and from the vegetable garden. As the smells emanated across the garden, we knew we were in for a dining treat that night. Recipe pictured on page 72.

2 teaspoons extra-virgin coconut oil
1 bay leaf
4–5 fresh or dried curry leaves, to taste
1 large brown onion, thinly sliced
½ teaspoon mustard seeds
¼ teaspoon fenugreek/methi seeds
1 tomato, roughly chopped
2 green finger chillies/chiles, finely chopped
¼–½ teaspoon chilli/chili powder, to taste
½ teaspoon ground turmeric
200 ml/scant 1 cup coconut milk
4 garlic bulbs (10–12 cloves per bulb), cloves all separated and peeled

SERVES 4–5 AS A SIDE DISH

Place a heavy-bottomed pan over medium heat and add the coconut oil. Add the bay leaf and curry leaves, then add the onion and fry gently for 6–8 minutes until well softened and starting to brown.

Add the mustard and fenugreek/methi seeds and, when they start to splutter, add the tomato, chillies/chiles, chilli/chili powder and ground turmeric. Turn down the heat to low and cook gently for 2 minutes.

Add the coconut milk and bring to a simmer. Add the garlic cloves and cook gently for 40 minutes until the garlic cloves are soft and sticky, but not completely falling apart. Add a few tablespoons of water, adding more if the gravy reduces too much.

Serve immediately alongside any curries.

Above: Snake beans, bitter melon/gourd, chillies/chilies, carrots and beetroot/beets at the vegetable market. Kandy, Sri Lanka.

SNAKE BEAN CURRY

250 g/9 oz. snake beans, or use green/French or runner beans
1 small red onion, finely chopped
2 small green finger chillies/chiles, finely chopped
1 teaspoon dried chilli flakes/ hot red pepper flakes
5–6 fresh or dried curry leaves
½ teaspoon ground turmeric
1 teaspoon ground cumin
½ teaspoon fennel powder
½ teaspoon fenugreek/methi seeds
1–2 teaspoons culinary/unflavoured coconut oil, or use good-quality vegetable oil (see page 13)

SERVES 4 AS A SIDE DISH

Another classic Sri Lankan dish, this curry is made with snake beans, sometimes called yardlong or asparagus beans. You can find this interesting tender vegetable in most Asian shops, as it's very popular across the continent. This bean can be easily substituted using green/French beans or runner beans. Traditionally, a little coconut cream is added at the end, but I prefer this dish served as a side dish of dry curry. Recipe pictured on page 72–73.

Top and tail the beans, and cut into 5-cm/2-in. pieces. Add to a large bowl, along with all the ingredients except the oil. Mix well so everything is combined.

Place a heavy-bottomed pan over high heat and add the oil. When the oil is hot, add the bean mixture and stir-fry for 5–6 minutes over very high heat, stirring well until the beans are tender.

Serve immediately with any curry and steamed red rice.

COCONUT ROTI

390 g/3 cups wholemeal/whole-wheat flour, plus extra for dusting
120 g/1½ cups desiccated/dried unsweetened shredded coconut
1 teaspoon salt
1 red onion, finely chopped
3 green chillies/chiles, thinly sliced
125 ml/½ cup coconut milk
2–4 teaspoons extra-virgin coconut oil, or use good-quality vegetable oil (see page 13)

MAKES 8

These simple rotis (pictured on page 73) make a tasty, crispy and nutty addition to any Sri Lankan meal. They are also also delicious for dessert, replacing the onions and chillies/chiles with chopped banana, and served with a drizzle of date syrup.

Mix together the flour, coconut and salt in a large bowl, then add the onion and chillies/chiles, mixing well. Make a well in the centre and pour in the coconut milk and 180 ml/¾ cup water. Combine to make a soft dough, adding more water if needed.

Knead the dough for a few minutes, then roll into a thick sausage shape. Break or cut into eight pieces and roll into balls. Place the balls on a sheet of parchment and cover with a damp cloth. Leave to rest for 30 minutes in a warm place.

Lightly flour a work surface and rolling pin. Roll out the balls of dough into 12.5–15-cm/5–6-in. rounds, about 3 mm/⅛ in. thick. Place a wide, non-stick frying pan/skillet over high heat and add a teaspoon of oil to coat the bottom of the pan. Place one roti in the pan, turn down the heat to medium and cook for 3 minutes on each side.

Wrap the cooked rotis in a kitchen towel to keep warm while cooking the rest. Add more oil to the pan as needed.

Serve immediately with any curries you like.

AMBUL POLOS
Green jackfruit curry

2 tablespoons extra-virgin coconut oil, or use good-quality vegetable oil (see page 13)

½ brown onion, finely chopped

2.5-cm/1-in. thumb of fresh ginger, peeled and finely chopped, or use 1 heaped tablespoon ginger paste

3 fat garlic cloves, finely chopped, or use 1 tablespoon garlic paste

8–10 fresh or dried curry leaves

5-cm/2-in. piece of pandan leaf, or use 1–2 drops pure vanilla extract (optional)

2 tablespoons roasted spice mix (see below)

1 teaspoon chilli/chili powder

½ teaspoon ground turmeric

1 teaspoon ground black pepper

7.5–10-cm/3–4-in. cinnamon stick

2 x 400-g/14-oz. cans green/young jackfruit, drained and rinsed

1 tablespoon tamarind pulp, or use ½ teaspoon tamarind concentrate plus 1 tablespoon water

1 teaspoon date syrup, or use pure maple syrup or unrefined coconut sugar

100 g/3½ oz. fresh coconut pieces (optional)

200 ml/scant 1 cup coconut milk

1 teaspoon salt, or to taste

SERVES 5–6

ROASTED SPICE MIX

2 tablespoons basmati rice

4 tablespoons coriander seeds

3 tablespoons cumin seeds

2 tablespoons black peppercorns

1 tablespoon mustard seeds

2 scant teaspoons green cardamom seeds (removed from pods)

1 teaspoon cloves (about 10 cloves)

1 heaped teaspoon fennel seeds

MAKES ABOUT 200 ML/SCANT 1 CUP

Jackfruit has clearly upped its marketing game, now appearing on street-food menus globally as an accessible alternative to meat. We had our first jackfruit curry in Sri Lanka, and I served it on my street-food menu for many years. The world's biggest tree fruit is now widely available in cans, either as a sweet ripe fruit or young and green to be used like a vegetable. It's important not to get the two types mixed up.

The star of this recipe is undoubtedly the roasted Sri Lankan spice mix, which you can find in specialist grocery shops, but it's quite simple to make your own and store in a sterilized jar for later use. You can use this spice base to make all manner of Sri Lankan-style curries, with whatever vegetables are in season. This recipe pairs deliciously with squashes, especially pumpkin. Or try simple sweet potato and chickpea/garbanzo bean. Serve with some Malay acar awak pickle (see page 161), which is very similar to Sri Lankan achcharu pickle, on the side or some date and lime chutney (see page 66) or spicy sambol.

For the roasted spice mix, toast the rice and spices for the mix in a dry frying pan/skillet, taking care not to burn them. It is easier to avoid burning by toasting the spices separately. Add them all to a mortar, food processor or spice grinder, and blend or grind until powdered. Store in a sterilized airtight container.

Place a pan over medium heat, add the coconut oil and onion, and sauté until softened, about 8–10 minutes. Add the ginger and garlic, and cook for a further 2 minutes. Now add the curry leaves and pandan leaf (if using), fry for 30 seconds and then add the roasted spice mix, chilli/chili powder, turmeric, black pepper and cinnamon, and combine well. Sauté for another few minutes, then add the jackfruit, tamarind and date syrup. Mix well, making sure the jackfruit pieces are well coated.

Finally add 125 ml/½ cup cold water, the coconut pieces and half the coconut milk, and bring to a simmer. Cook gently for about 45 minutes until the jackfruit is well softened. Add a little more water if needed, and season with salt to taste. Add the remaining coconut milk just before serving and mix well.

Serve with steamed red rice for a nutty, wholegrain accompaniment and some chutney or spicy sambol on the side, if you like.

SPICED CARROT & PINEAPPLE CAKE

Sri Lankan pineapples are a popular ingredient in Sri Lanka, and the local spices and pineapples make a perfect pairing for carrot cake. Using flours higher in nut protein – and reducing the more refined sugars by adding extra fruit for sweetness – this lightly spiced cake has a tropical feel and will satisfy sweet cravings, as well as providing a little helping of nutrients.

Preheat the oven to 170°C (340°F) Gas 4.

Mix together the soya/soy milk, oil, vinegar, coconut sugar and maple syrup in a large bowl and leave to curdle for 5 minutes.

Sift the plain/all-purpose flour (or gluten-free flour and xanthan gum) into a separate bowl, then add the blanched ground almonds and coconut flour, if using. Add the salt, baking powder, bicarbonate of soda/baking soda and all the dry spices. Mix together well.

Combine the milk and oil mixture with the dry ingredients, adding it gradually but mixing quickly, and making sure there are no lumps in the batter. Then add the grated carrot, crushed pineapple, vanilla and three-quarters of the walnut pieces, mixing together quickly again.

Divide the batter between the cake pans. Place in the preheated oven immediately and bake until they are evenly risen and cooked through, about 35–40 minutes, or until a skewer inserted comes out clean. Run a knife around edge of the cake pans and turn the cakes out onto wire racks to cool completely.

To make the cashew frosting, blend the soaked cashews and yogurt until they form a smooth cream. Add the maple syrup, lemon juice, vanilla and salt, then blend again. Add a spoonful of water if needed – the cashew frosting should be very thick but spreadable.

Using a palette knife or metal spatula, stack the sponges, spreading a generous layer of frosting between each layer. Cover the outside and top of the cake with frosting, too. Sprinkle with the remaining walnuts. You can pipe some of the leftover frosting on top and add whatever decorations you like, such as candied pineapple pieces. Place in the fridge until needed.

250 ml/1 cup unsweetened soya/ soy milk
250 ml/1 cup coconut oil, melted, or use plain vegetable oil
½ tablespoon apple cider vinegar
115 g/¾ cup coconut sugar
60 ml/¼ cup pure maple syrup, or use date syrup
125 g/1 cup plain/all-purpose flour, or use 125 g/scant ¾ cup gluten-free flour plus ¾ teaspoon xanthan gum
165 g/1⅔ cups blanched ground almonds
55 g/½ cup coconut flour, or use an extra 100 g/1 cup blanched ground almonds
¾ teaspoon salt
2 teaspoons baking powder
2 teaspoons bicarbonate of soda/ baking soda
1½ tablespoons ground ginger
1 scant tablespoon ground cinnamon
¼ teaspoon ground nutmeg
¼ teaspoon ground cloves
280 g/2 cups grated carrot (about 3 carrots)
about 250 ml/1 cup crushed pineapple (use a 240-g/8-oz. can of 4 rings, juice drained and blended, or 120 g/ 4 oz. fresh pineapple, blended)
½ teaspoon vanilla bean paste, or use 1 teaspoon pure vanilla extract or seeds of ½ vanilla pod/bean
125 g/1 cup walnut pieces

CASHEW FROSTING
240 g/2 cups cashew nuts, soaked in cold water overnight
215 g/1 cup coconut yogurt
1½ teaspoons pure maple syrup
1 tablespoon freshly squeezed lemon juice
¼ teaspoon vanilla bean paste, or use 1 teaspoon pure vanilla extract
pinch of salt
candied pineapple pieces, to decorate (optional)

4 round cake pans, 15 cm/6 in. diameter, lightly oiled and base-lined

SERVES 8–10

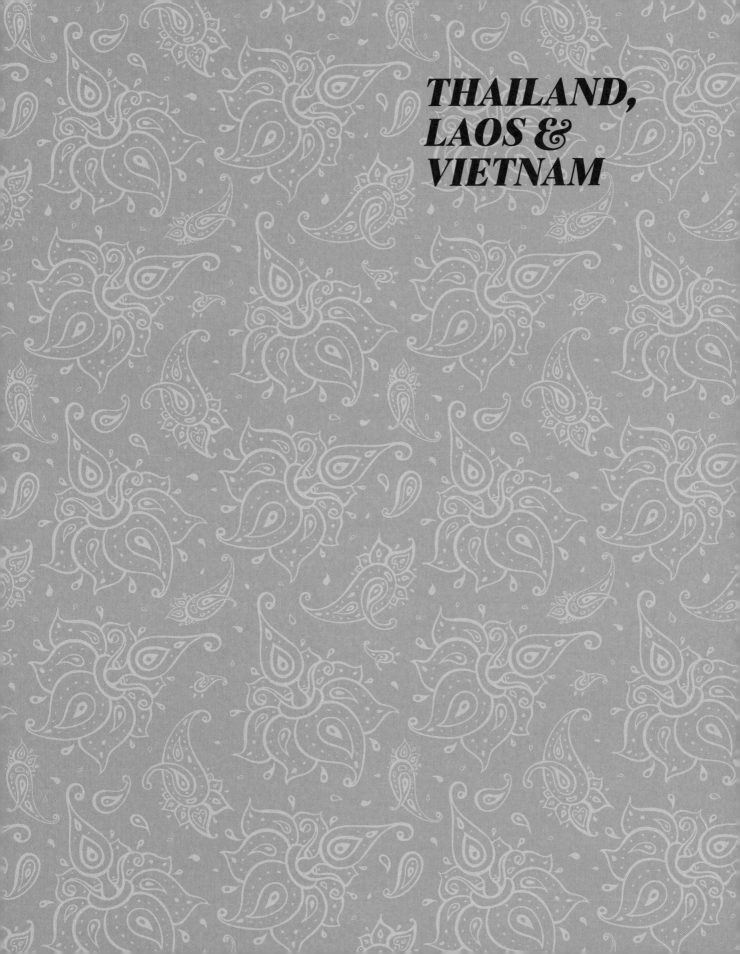

THAILAND, LAOS & VIETNAM

Thailand

There were almost 30 years between my first and most recent trip to Thailand, and our last few visits have been highly contrasting, from luxury hideaway retreats on remote corners of luscious islands to exploring somewhat lesser known corners. A timespan like that affords you some witness to change in all kinds of aspects. The country is certainly wealthier than those early days, with a now well established middle class. And in terms of tourism, has tried to shed a little of its backpacker identity and is now home to many upscale retreats. On our last trip, we still managed to spend several months travelling almost as cheaply as we did back in the early 90s. Simple rooms, surface travel by bus and train, although we did upgrade our last overnight train to first class. I had been hoping for train food reminiscent of those early journeys, but sadly that was no longer the case. However, what hasn't changed are the food sellers scattered along the platforms and the little bags of ready to eat fritters, dips and prepared fruit. Some stations even have rather impromptu set ups of stools and street food, where you can slurp up some noodles whilst waiting for your train. We are now well practised on long train journeys, never short on snacks and light meals, and ready to stock up at station stops whenever the opportunity arises.

Having done our fair share of lazing the days away on idyllic islands, and trekking through dense interiors, we decided to follow the road less travelled through the north-east regions on our latest trip. With several old friends now living there, it seemed like the perfect excuse to plan a route around that. We linked bus routes from Bangkok, winding our way up through the Isan regions of Kalasin, Sakon Nakon and Udon Thani, then looping across through prehistoric-looking national parks to our favourite

Phitsanulok, with its hub of markets and incredible food (probably due to its central location across several arterial routes for northern and eastern Thailand). As we were planning a little luxury later in Vietnam, we stuck to mostly $20-a-night guesthouses or cheap hotels. At one point, we found ourselves in Khon Kaen staying next to a Correctional Institution for Drug Addicts, waking up early to loudspeaker-led meditation and exercise. This was also a university town, so the streets were filled with cafés, street carts and a buzzing nightly street food market. I was quite happy to wake up early as there was much to explore and eat. The town also boasted a dedicated vegan food hall, which we haunted on several occasions, as it was such a joy to come across one that is solely plant-based. As you enter the hall, you purchase your tickets at the entrance desk and then simply wander up to the different counters to choose whatever you like the look of. It's the kind of place that makes you wish you had a bigger stomach. There are food halls at both Bangkok's airports, but I can tell you now it's a quite a challenge to find vegan food in these generic halls and you definitely need to be equipped with a few Thai words to get by.

Between journeys, we spent our days with friends learning about what it's really like to live and work there. One friend grows organic mushrooms, another rescues 'soi' street dogs and another teaches English to devoted young students. It was quite a surprise to find that my particular MasterChef series was very popular in Thailand and I even had a few local fans. So we collected mushrooms from their farm and threw a little impromptu BBQ party. I showed them some easy marinades for skewers and how I make vegan laab from mushrooms, and they taught us how to barbeque sticky rice cakes, whilst we all sang Oasis songs. Our friends showed

us around bustling markets and took us to explore corners we may never have otherwise found. One of these gems was a monastery that looks after older people with no family. They grow their own produce and sell wondrous creams and herbal potions, herbs and spices, fragrant natural soaps and even the best vegan fermented 'fish' paste I've ever tasted. I realise now I should have bought more jars to bring home.

Surface travel in Thailand is by far the best way to see the changing landscape and explore the diversity of food, from the northern and eastern heavily forested mountainous regions, down through bustling Bangkok and to the winding south with its ancient limestone karsts that rise up from nowhere like prehistoric monoliths, surrounded by pristine rainforests and the sounds of waterfalls and gibbon calls. Although most tourists are heading straight for the powdery sandy beaches and dreamy hideaway islands, there are always hidden gems that justify leaving that beaten track.

Clockwise from top left: Fishermen at sunset, Bangrak Port, Koh Samui; Cluster of electricity wires, Bangkok; Buddhist statue in Sukhothai Historic Park, Mueang Kao; Longtail boats amongst the Thonburi canals of Bangkok.

KHAO TOM
Fragrant breakfast soup with rice

1 tablespoon good-quality vegetable oil
(see page 13)

2 banana shallots, finely chopped,
or use 1 small brown onion

240 g/2 cups cooked brown basmati rice,
or use any leftover cooked rice

1 carrot, peeled and cut into 1-cm/½-in.
cubes

5 chestnut/cremini mushrooms,
cut into 1-cm/½-in. cubes

½ small turnip or swede, peeled and cut
into 1-cm/½-in. cubes

1 stick of celery, cut into 1-cm/½-in. cubes

2 stems purple sprouting broccoli,
cut into small florets, no bigger than
2 cm/¾ in. (reserve stems for stock,
below)

¼ cauliflower, cut into small florets,
no bigger than 2 cm/¾ in. (reserve
stems for stock, below)

large handful of black kale (cavalo nero), or
use any dark cabbage, roughly chopped

handful of coriander/cilantro, to serve

2–3 spring onions/scallions, thinly sliced
at an angle, to serve

2–3 hot chillies/chiles, thinly sliced,
in rice vinegar (optional)

lime wedges, to serve

STOCK

vegetable stems from the trimmed
broccoli and/or cauliflower

2 lemongrass sticks, crushed and chopped

1 tablespoon Korean fermented soya
bean/soybean paste (doenjang),
or use brown or red miso paste

2–3 teaspoons good-quality vegetable
stock powder/bouillon

CRISPY GARLIC AND ONIONS

250 ml/1 cup good-quality vegetable oil
(see page 13), for frying, plus extra if
needed

1 garlic bulb, cloves separated and
finely chopped

1 small brown onion, thinly sliced

SERVES 4

Khao tom is a flavoursome Thai-style vegetable and rice soup, traditionally eaten at breakfast, using leftover cooked rice (but you can also cook the rice in the broth). The vegetables can be easily adjusted to seasonal produce, as well as your own personal favourites. I find this a fantastic start to the day, especially when I've woken up hungry or haven't eaten well the day before. It's also the perfect antidote to cold and gloomy mornings in winter.

My recipe here also includes the method for making crispy garlic and onions, which can be prepared in advance and stored in an airtight container. This is a key ingredient in Thai and South-East Asian cooking, and makes a flavourful topping for noodles and soups.

Add all the stock ingredients to a large pan with 2 litres/quarts water and bring to the boil. Reduce to a simmer and cook for 10–15 minutes, then remove from the heat and leave to cool. Pour the stock through a sieve/strainer into a jug/pitcher, removing the stems and lemongrass.

Place the empty pan back over medium heat. Add the oil and shallots and fry for 10–15 minutes until translucent. Set aside.

For the crispy garlic, add the oil to a small frying pan/skillet. Add the garlic to the cool oil and then place over medium–high heat. When the garlic starts to fry, stir well and reduce the heat to low. Keep stirring and frying gently until eventually the garlic starts to turn golden brown. Turn off the heat. Remove with a slotted spoon and drain on paper towels.

Place the same pan of oil back over medium–high heat and then add the sliced onion (top up the oil if needed). Fry until the onion is deep golden brown and crispy. Remove with a slotted spoon and drain on paper towels. Set aside.

Add the strained stock and cooked rice to the shallot pan, and bring to a simmer (if using uncooked rice, cook over medium heat for 10 minutes until about 75 per cent cooked). Add the chopped vegetables (except the kale), 1 tablespoon of the crispy garlic and simmer for another 7–8 minutes until the vegetables are just tender and the rice is fully cooked. Add the kale and stir well for another minute or so. Add a little more water if needed.

To serve, add some rice and vegetables to a deep bowl, top up with broth and sprinkle with crispy garlic and onions, coriander/cilantro and spring onions/scallions. Serve with pickled chillies/chiles, if using, and lime wedges on the side.

STUFFED CUCUMBER SOUP

4–5 fat garlic cloves, to taste, or use 4–5 teaspoons garlic paste

2.5-cm/1-in. thumb of fresh ginger, peeled, or use 1 heaped tablespoon of ginger paste

3–4 coriander/cilantro roots, or use small handful of stems plus 1 tablespoon of freshly chopped leaves

1 heaped teaspoon white peppercorns, roughly ground or crushed

120 g/4 oz. tempeh

1 tablespoon rice flour

1 tablespoon soy sauce, or use tamari or coconut aminos for gluten-free

¼ teaspoon salt

2 small cucumbers, or use 1 large

BROTH

1 litre/quart good-quality vegetable stock

1 tablespoon vegan fish sauce (see page 13), or use ½ tablespoon soy sauce or tamari

¼ teaspoon coconut sugar, or use date syrup or maple syrup

1 tablespoon soy sauce, or use tamari or coconut aminos for gluten-free

¼ teaspoon freshly ground white pepper

salt, to taste

1 spring onion/scallion, thinly sliced, to serve

small handful of coriander/cilantro, to serve

SERVES 4 AS AN ACCOMPANIMENT, OR 2 AS A LIGHT MEAL

This classic Thai soup is easily made vegan, and makes a great light lunch or can be served traditionally as a light backdrop in a Thai banquet. My favourite version, usually made with stuffed bitter melon/gourd, is served at Mai's Veggie Café, probably one of the best vegan restaurants in Bangkok. Wherever I'm staying, I always travel across the city to Sukhumvit to enjoy a vegan feast at Mai's. Now that my Khao San and Banglamphu backpacker days are long gone, I prefer to stay near the south-west river loop or Chinatown. If you like to shop, then Sukhumvit might be more up your street.

Place the garlic, ginger, coriander/cilantro roots (or stems if using) and roughly ground peppercorns in a small food processor or blender (or jug/pitcher with stick blender) and blend to a paste. Alternatively, use a pestle and mortar and grind until you get a rough paste – which is an easier method for this small quantity. Place the paste in a medium bowl, and crumble the tempeh into the mixture. Add the rice flour, soy sauce and salt, and mix well.

Lightly peel the cucumber(s) so the skin still has a few green stripes on it, then slice into 2.5-cm/1-in. thick slices and use a small paring knife to carefully remove the seeds in the middle. Arrange the slices onto a large plate, and stuff the holes with the tempeh mixture, pressing it in firmly. Once all the cucumber pieces have been stuffed, place the plate into the fridge to set for at least 30 minutes.

For the broth, in a large saucepan, add the vegetable stock, vegan fish sauce, coconut sugar and soy sauce. Bring to a simmer, then gently add the stuffed cucumber pieces. Cover the pan and poach gently over low heat for 10 minutes.

Add the ground white pepper and taste the stock. Add salt to taste, but remember it is intended to have a very light taste and serves as a great palate cleanser during the meal. Gently place the stuffed cucumber pieces into small bowls and pour over the broth. Sprinkle with spring onion/scallion slices and coriander/cilantro. Serve immediately.

YUM SOM O
Pomelo salad with crispy enoki mushrooms

½ pomelo (about 250 g/9 oz.)

5 tablespoons coarse desiccated/dried unsweetened shredded coconut, lightly toasted

4 tablespoons unsalted peanuts, lightly toasted and roughly chopped

2 banana shallots, thinly sliced, or use 1 small red onion

¼ lemongrass stick, plump end, sliced and finely chopped

2 kaffir lime leaves, very thinly sliced

1–2 red chillies/chiles, to taste, finely chopped

small handful of freshly chopped mint leaves

small handful of freshly chopped coriander/cilantro

1 tablespoon crispy onions (see page 82, optional)

10 spinach leaves, about 7.5–10 cm/3–4 in., to serve, or use massaged kale leaves

SAUCE

2–3 dried red chillies/chiles, lightly toasted

freshly squeezed juice of 2 small limes

1 tablespoon date syrup, or use unrefined brown sugar

2 tablespoons tamarind pulp, or use 1 teaspoon tamarind concentrate plus 1½ tbsp water

2 tablespoons vegan fish sauce (see page 13), or use soy sauce or tamari

CRISPY MUSHROOMS

100 g/3½ oz. enoki mushrooms, or use any mushrooms you have

½ tablespoon soy sauce, or use tamari or coconut aminos for gluten-free

1 tablespoon cornflour/cornstarch

2 tablespoons culinary/unflavoured coconut oil, melted, or use good-quality vegetable oil (see page 13)

baking sheet, lined with parchment

SERVES 4–5 AS SMALL PLATES

Oh pomelo, we love you so! Ancestor to the humble grapefruit and native to South-East Asia, pomelo is easy to find in Asian stores, and sometimes in supermarkets/grocery stores during the European winter when it's in season. It's less acidic and slightly sweeter than grapefruit, but pink grapefruit makes an okay substitute. Pomelo are also less juicy, so they work well in salads, and the segments are easier to separate.

Yum translates as 'mixed together' or 'tossed', so you can make yum out of anything. My recipe includes mushrooms and utilizes a good vegan fish sauce (see page 13). This recipe captures the classic flavour balance of Thai food – sweet, sour, salty and spicy, combined with different textures. It makes a great starter or light lunch. Spinach or kale leaves make a good alternative to betel leaves. Recipe pictured on page 88.

For the sauce, break the toasted chillies/chiles into pieces, place in a mortar and grind with a pestle. Add the lime juice, date syrup, tamarind and vegan fish sauce. Continue to grind until you have a well-blended sauce. Set aside.

Preheat the oven to 210°C (400°F) Gas 6.

For the crispy mushrooms, separate the individual enoki mushrooms, and slice any thicker parts of stem into small strips. If using other mushrooms, slice into small strips/pieces. Toss the mushroom pieces in the soy sauce and then the cornflour/cornstarch. Arrange on the lined baking sheet and drizzle with the oil. (You can also use an air-fryer for this step, or shallow-fry, baking in the oven will achieve the crispiest texture.) Bake in the preheated oven for 20–25 minutes until browning and crispy. Transfer to paper towels and set aside.

Prepare the pomelo, by removing the skin and all the pith. Separate the flesh from the segments. The flesh can be in different sized pieces, from small strips to slightly larger chunks up to 2-cm/¾-in. in size. Add the remaining salad ingredients (except the spinach leaves) into a large bowl along with the pomelo pieces. Mix well, then pour over the sauce and combine.

Pile the salad onto a plate and top with the mushrooms. Trim the stems from the spinach leaves and serve alongside. To eat, spoon some salad into a leaf and roll up like a stuffed pancake.

Left: Fruit and flower vendor at a floating market, Bangkok.

MASSAMAN CURRY IN A HURRY *with mushrooms, sweet potato & peanuts*

40 g/1½ oz. TVP chunks
1 teaspoon yeast extract
500 ml/2 cups vegetable stock, or use water
1 teaspoon extra-virgin coconut oil
seeds of 2 cardamom pods
7.5–10-cm/3–4-in. cinnamon stick
2–3 whole cloves, to taste
1 star anise
½ teaspoon ground cumin (if not listed as an ingredient in the ready-made paste)
4 tablespoons red curry paste
¼ teaspoon ground/grated nutmeg
1 teaspoon Korean fermented soya bean/soybean paste (doenjang), or use brown or red miso paste
½ teaspoon salt, or to taste
¼ teaspoon ground black pepper
1 sweet potato, peeled and cut into 2.5-cm/1-in. cubes (about 350 g/ 3 cups), or use skin-on new potatoes
200 g/7 oz. chestnut/cremini mushrooms, quartered
400-ml/14-oz. can coconut milk
45 g/⅓ cup unsalted peanuts, lightly toasted and roughly chopped
freshly chopped coriander/cilantro, to garnish
1 red chilli/chile, thinly sliced, to garnish

SERVES 4

This crowd-pleasing curry has an intriguing history. Also known as matsuman or mussulman (an old word for Muslim), this curry hails from the Ayutthaya court in central Thailand during the early 1600s, and is said to have Persian origins. That said, many see this as a dish from southern Thailand, due to the influence of their Malaysian neighbours, whose own cuisine has been heavily influenced by the Indian spice trail. This explains the kind of spices you will find in massaman – a little different to the usual Thai repertoire – including cumin, cloves, nutmeg, cinnamon, cardamom and star anise.

This recipe is a slightly cheat-y version using ready-made Thai red curry paste, and adding some extra missing spices at the start. You can of course make the spice paste base from scratch, but red curry paste is so widely available, and very easy to adapt to make this dish more easily at home. Recipe pictured on page 89.

Place the TVP chunks in a bowl with the yeast extract, 1 teaspoon of the vegetable stock and enough boiling water to cover. Allow to soak for 20 minutes.

Place a large wok or frying pan/skillet over high heat. Add the coconut oil, cardamom seeds, cinnamon, cloves and star anise. Toast for 1–2 minutes until the aromas are released. Now add the ground cumin, if using, and toast for a further 30 seconds.

Add the red curry paste, and fry for 1–2 minutes, then add the remaining vegetable stock or water. Bring to a simmer and add the TVP, its soaking water, the nutmeg, Korean fermented soya bean/soybean paste, salt, pepper, sweet potato and mushrooms. Simmer gently over low–medium heat for 10 minutes until the potatoes are soft (longer if using new potatoes).

Add the coconut milk and roughly chopped peanuts (keeping a tablespoon back to garnish), then season with more salt to taste, if needed. Garnish with the remaining peanuts, fresh coriander/ cilantro and sliced chilli/chile. Serve with steamed black rice and coconut roti (see page 71).

TOM KHA
Thai fragrant coconut soup

This crowd-pleasing and healthy soup can be found on Thai menus across Europe. It's very easy to prepare in less than 20 minutes and perfect for a comforting and nourishing light meal. That's faster than the delivery company will get this to you from your local Thai restaurant.

You can make this soup with any veggies you have. I like to add some greens, like spinach and broccoli. It's important to include a good protein (this dish traditionally features chicken), such as tofu/beancurd or vegan chicken, but mushrooms work well on their own too. Recipe pictured on page 89.

Place a heavy-bottomed pan or wok over medium heat and add the coconut oil. Add the shallots and fry for 3–4 minutes until translucent, but not starting to colour, then add the chillies/chiles. Stir-fry for another 1–2 minutes.

Cut each lemongrass stick into 2 or 3 smaller sticks. Using a rolling pin or the back of a heavy knife, bruise the lemongrass well to release the fragrant aromas, then place in the pan along with the kaffir lime leaves and galangal. Keep cooking for another few minutes, so all the aromatics are well combined and fragrant. Add the garlic slices and cook for 1 minute, stirring well.

Add 800 ml/scant 3½ cups water to the pan, along with the coconut milk, soya bean/soybean paste, date syrup and vegan fish sauce. Reduce the heat, and simmer very gently on the lowest heat for 5 minutes. Remove the lemongrass sticks.

Add the mushrooms, broccoli and tofu/beancurd, and gently simmer for another 5 minutes until the broccoli is just tender. Stir in the baby spinach leaves. Remove from the heat and check the seasoning, adding a little salt or soy sauce, if you like.

Serve immediately with freshly torn herbs and lime wedges.

½ tablespoon extra-virgin coconut oil

2 banana shallots, or 1 small brown onion, finely chopped

2–4 red chillies/chiles, to taste, finely chopped

2 lemongrass sticks, trimmed

6–8 fresh or dried kaffir lime leaves

5-cm/2-in. thumb of fresh galangal, peeled and sliced into 3-mm/⅛-in. thick discs, or use ginger

3–4 fat garlic cloves, to taste, thinly sliced

400-ml/14-oz. can coconut milk

1 tablespoon Korean fermented soya bean/soybean paste (doenjang), or use brown or red miso paste

1 teaspoon date syrup, or use pure maple syrup or coconut sugar

1 tablespoon vegan fish sauce (see page 13), or use soy sauce or tamari

200 g/7 oz. oyster mushrooms, torn into large strips

200 g/7 oz. broccoli, cut into small florets, or use cauliflower

200g/7 oz. firm tofu/beancurd, cut into 2-cm/¾-in. pieces, or use vegan 'chicken' pieces

100 g/2 cups baby spinach, roughly torn, or use larger spinach or chard

salt, to taste, or use soy sauce, tamari or coconut aminos

small handful of freshly torn Thai basil, or use European basil (optional), to serve

small handful of freshly torn coriander/cilantro, to serve

lime wedges, to serve

SERVES 4

PAD MED MA MUANG LETTUCE CUPS
Thai-style stir-fry with vegetables & cashews

I know I should eat more raw food, but it's so challenging when the weather is colder. It's easy to order a salad when I'm lounging on a Thai island or stalking the sweaty streets of Bangkok. This classic Thai stir-fry only lightly cooks the veggies, so it's almost as good as eating raw. Served in lettuce cups for a light and crunchy alternative to rice, these tasty little boats are deceptively filling. And it's almost a salad, right?

All the effort is in the vegetable prep for this dish. You can use whatever seasonal veg you have, but crunchy vegetables work best in this dish, so it's important not to overcook them. Once prepped, this dish can be on the table in less than 15 minutes.

Place a wok or large frying pan/skillet over high heat. Add the roughly torn chillies/chiles (including seeds if you want to keep it spicy), and lightly toast until just starting to change colour. Remove from the pan and set aside.

Add the oil to the hot pan, then add the swede, mooli/daikon, carrot, celery, courgette/zucchini and (bell) pepper. Stir-fry for 5–6 minutes over very high heat, mixing well, until the veg starts to colour. Now add the garlic and toasted chilli/chile pieces, and stir-fry for another 1–2 minutes until the garlic is just cooked.

Add the cabbage, then add all the sauce ingredients, along with 2 tablespoons water. Cook over high heat for 1–2 minutes until sizzling hot. Add the cashews and the spring onion/scallion whites, and mix well until everything is well coated in the sauce. Add a little more water if needed. Remove from the heat.

To serve, arrange the lettuce cups on a platter, and fill with the stir-fry mixture. Top with the spring onion/scallion greens, coriander/cilantro and chilli/chile slices. Serve immediately.

7 dried red chillies/chiles, roughly torn
½ tablespoon culinary/unflavoured coconut oil, or use good-quality vegetable oil (see page 13)
200 g/7 oz. swede or turnip, peeled and cut into 1-cm/½-in. cubes
7.5-cm/3-in. piece of mooli/daikon radish, peeled and cut into 1-cm/½-in. cubes
1 carrot, peeled and cut into 1-cm/½-in. cubes
2 sticks of celery, cut into 1-cm/½-in. cubes
1 courgette/zucchini, cut into 1-cm/½-in. cubes
½ red or green (bell) pepper, cut into 1-cm/½-in. cubes
2 fat garlic cloves, finely chopped, or use 2 teaspoons garlic paste
140 g/4½ oz. Chinese cabbage (about ¼ cabbage), cut into 5-cm/2-in. pieces, or use white cabbage
120 g/1 cup cashew nuts, lightly toasted
2 spring onions/scallions, thinly sliced and separated into white and green parts

SAUCE
2 tablespoons vegan 'oyster' sauce, aka mushroom stir-fry sauce
2 teaspoons soy sauce, or use tamari or coconut aminos for gluten-free
2 teaspoons dark soy sauce, or use tamari for gluten-free
2 teaspoons date syrup, or use pure maple syrup or coconut sugar

TO SERVE
1 Little Gem/Bibb lettuce, leaves separated into cups
coriander/cilantro
1 red chilli/chile, thinly sliced

SERVES 4

THAI 'CRAB' RICE WITH GREEN SAUCE

Take a wander down Yaowarat Street in Bangkok after dark and you will find yourself immersed in a bustling street-food market with seemingly endless seafood (and the occasional veggie and vegan offering). It's an exciting area to take in the energetic and pungent atmosphere of this Chinese Thai market area with its alleyways for days. The green sauce is served as a dipping condiment for large shellfish and also on the side of Bangkok's famous Crab-fried Rice. There are cafés and restaurants in Thailand that specialize only in this dish. That surely must warrant a vegan version.

To make an authentic textured sauce, you will need to use a pestle and mortar, and pound all the green sauce ingredients, except the liquids, to make a coarse paste. Then add the liquids and pound some more. (You can use a food processor or blender, if you prefer, but it's a thick sauce in a small quantity, so a pestle and mortar, stick blender or spice grinder works best.) Cover and set aside.

Prepare the palm hearts by rinsing well, slicing lengthways and then removing the centre parts. Place the centre parts in a sieve/strainer over a bowl. Slice the remaining long pieces each into 4 x 1-cm/1½ x ½-in. strips and add to the sieve/strainer.

Place a wok or large frying pan/skillet over medium heat and add the oil and garlic. Fry the garlic until it's almost golden brown, moving it around the pan so it doesn't burn. Crumble the tofu/beancurd into the pan, and fry for another 2–3 minutes until the tofu/beancurd starts to brown around the edges, then add the rice and mix together really well.

Turn up the heat to high and fry the rice mixture for about 2–3 minutes, turning regularly by tossing the pan or using a spatula. Add the soy sauce, vegan fish sauce, date syrup, white pepper and salt. Mix well. Now add the palm hearts and spring onion/scallion whites, and gently mix into the rice whilst cooking over medium–high heat, for approximately 2–3 minutes.

Line one side of the plate with sliced cucumber, arrange the rice on the plate and top with coriander/cilantro leaves, the spring onion/scallion greens and some lime slices. Serve with green sauce on the side.

120 g/4 oz. palm hearts
2 tablespoons culinary/unflavoured coconut oil, or use good-quality vegetable oil (see page 13)
5 fat garlic cloves, finely chopped, or use 5 teaspoons garlic paste
170 g/6 oz. firm tofu/beancurd
300 g/2½ cups cooled steamed jasmine or basmati rice (from the day before is better)
1 tablespoon soy sauce, or use tamari or coconut aminos for gluten-free
1 tablespoon vegan fish sauce (see page 13)
½ teaspoon date syrup, or use pure maple syrup or coconut sugar
¼ teaspoon white pepper
large pinch of salt
2 spring onions/scallions, thinly sliced at an angle and separated into white and green parts
¼ cucumber, roughly peeled and sliced, to serve
small handful of coriander/cilantro, to serve
lime slices, to serve

GREEN SAUCE
6 fat garlic cloves
2 coriander/cilantro roots, or use a small handful of fresh coriander/cilantro stems
small handful of Thai sweet basil leaves, or use whatever basil you have
4–8 small green chillies/chiles, to taste
large pinch of salt
1 tablespoon date syrup, or use pure maple syrup or coconut sugar
2 tablespoons vegan fish sauce (see page 13), or use soy sauce or tamari
freshly squeezed juice of ½ lime (about 2 tablespoons)
2 tablespoons rice vinegar (or, even better, use the pickling vinegar from a jar of pickled chillies/chiles, radishes or garlic, if you have some)

SERVES 4 AS AN ACCOMPANIMENT

RAW 'PAD THAI'

1 large or 2 small–medium
    courgettes/zucchini
2 small–medium carrots, peeled
120 g/4 oz. firm tofu/beancurd,
    roughly crumbled
1 tablespoon choi poh/preserved
    radish, finely chopped (optional)
35 g/¼ cup unsalted peanuts, lightly
    toasted
large handful of beansprouts
small handful of coriander/cilantro
2 spring onions/scallions, thinly sliced
    at an angle
1 tablespoon pumpkin seeds, soaked
    for 1 hour, then drained and lightly
    toasted, to serve
2 large red chillies/chiles, thinly sliced
    at an angle
lime wedges, to serve

SAUCE
3 tablespoons tamarind pulp, or use
    1½ tsp tamarind concentrate plus
    2 tbsp water
1 tablespoon vegan fish sauce
    (see page 13), or use extra soy sauce
2 tablespoons soy sauce, or use tamari
    or coconut aminos for gluten-free
2 tablespoons date syrup, or use pure
    maple syrup or coconut sugar

SERVES 2

This recipe title is somewhat of a misnomer, since pad means 'fried or stir-fried' in Thai. For me, a good pad Thai is the prince of Thai street food. It's the dish that got me through an early MasterChef invention test, even after I dropped my pan on the floor and had to start again. Mainly achieved because I had some sauce left, and if you've prepped your sauce well, everything else will fall into place.

Since my last few visits to Thailand, and the rise of the wellness retreat, raw 'pad Thai' is now very much a thing. My first thought was that it would be like a fancy salad, but it actually works brilliantly as a raw food dish that tingles your tastebuds and leaves you happily satiated. Choi poh, or preserved radish, comes in small packets, and adds that pungent radish note essential to a good pad Thai. But you could also simply add some extra fresh mooli/daikon strips to the vegetable mix.

Using a spiralizer, mandoline or julienne vegetable tool, slice the courgette(s)/zucchini and carrots into long spaghetti-like strips. Place in a large bowl and set aside.

Mix the sauce ingredients together and taste to check the balance of sweet, sour and salty flavours. Adjust if needed.

Add the sauce, tofu/beancurd and choi poh (if using) to the vegetable bowl and, using your hands, mix well until everything is well coated in the sauce. Allow to marinate for 5–10 minutes, then add the peanuts and beansprouts, and mix well.

Pile the salad onto a large plate and top with coriander/cilantro, spring onions/scallions, pumpkin seeds and chillies/chiles. Serve with lime wedges on the side.

SOUTHERN-STYLE SOUR BAMBOO SHOOT CURRY

I always promised myself once I became a confident snorkeller and free diver, I would actually learn to dive. I lined up a trip for my 50th birthday and headed out to start an extended South-East Asian trip with my husband Lee, starting with a diving course. After a 3-day overland journey to reach the northern shores of Ko Pha Ngan, I dropped my rucksack on the floor of what would be our new home for a month. A tiny mint green stilted Thai house, set amongst the jungle and coconut forest, with a tiny winding path that went over a rickety bridge and emerged onto an empty white sand beach, complete with rolling azure surf and Thai fishing boats chugging across the bay.

Then I received a phone call from my sister and had to fly home immediately for a family emergency. Trip (and diving) postponed indefinitely. Once I had lined up emergency flights back to Bangkok from the neighbouring island of Ko Samui, we headed out to eat for our one evening in this charming old fishing village. I knew where I was going as I'd been here two years earlier. And hopefully I'll get to go back one day.

The woman who makes this dish has been cooking from her little street shack restaurant for decades. I know this because my best friend has been coming here since she lived on the island as a youngster, and she's the same age as me. That's how I came to be here. And why I won't name the village. Because sometimes we 'farangs' really ruin things. I'm acutely aware that change and development is inevitable. But it didn't stop my sharp intake of breath when my boat arrived at Thong Sala port. My previous visit to this island had involved stepping off a tiny boat carrying around 20 or so people onto a short wooden pier. You could still see the rickety degraded remnants of the structure further down the bay, but this time, I stepped off a large passenger ferry onto a blazing-hot concrete pier with covered waiting areas full of plastic seats, 4-wheel-drive pick-ups with blacked-out screens chauffeuring linen-clad Instagram influencer squads to their glam pads... and the inescapable scabby dog or two.

I walked down the pier into town and stalled as I tried to find my bearings. Roundabouts, dual carriageways, multi-storey buildings. This was not the island I visited some 25 years ago. And how much was I part of that change? A question all travellers have to ask themselves if they want to tread more lightly.

This dish is one of my favourite light-prep Thai-style curries. I have to say style here, as I've tried to replicate a curry I've eaten quite a few times, but have never seen a recipe for. I'm not sure if it even has a name, or it's just one of this marvellous cook's creations with simple accessible ingredients. Either way, I've got pretty close here. Sour, spicy, fragrant broth with soft soup-plumped tofu/beancurd and crunchy bamboo shoots. What's not to love?

300 g/10½ oz. firm tofu/beancurd,
   cut into small rectangles
½–1 tablespoon culinary/unflavoured
   coconut oil, or use good-quality
   vegetable oil (see page 13)
4 fat garlic cloves, finely chopped,
   or use 4 teaspoons garlic paste
   (but it won't be as delicious as freshly
   made crispy garlic)
4-cm/1½-in. thumb of fresh ginger,
   peeled and finely chopped, or use
   2 tablespoons ginger paste
1–2 tablespoons sambol olek, or use
   any good-quality hot chilli/chili paste
   (preferably without sugar)
800 ml/scant 3½ cups vegetable stock
2 tablespoons tamarind pulp, or
   1 teaspoon tamarind concentrate
   plus 1½ tablespoons water
freshly squeezed juice of ½ lime
2–3 fresh or dried kaffir lime leaves,
   to taste
2 tablespoons soy sauce, or use tamari
   or coconut aminos for gluten-free
¼ teaspoon salt, or to taste
225-g/8-oz. can or jar bamboo shoots,
   rinsed and drained
large handful of beansprouts, or use
   ½ jar or can if you can't get fresh
12–20 Thai basil leaves, to taste,
   or use whatever basil you have
lime wedges, to serve
1–2 red chilli(es)/chile(s), thinly sliced
   and covered with rice vinegar,
   to serve (optional)

baking sheet, lined with parchment

SERVES 3–4

If you like your tofu/beancurd with more texture, preheat the oven to 170°C (340°F) Gas 4 and arrange the tofu/beancurd pieces on the lined baking sheet. Bake in the preheated oven for 15–20 minutes until slightly crisped. Alternatively, just add the pieces to the wok halfway through frying the garlic.

Place a wok over medium heat and add the coconut oil and garlic. Fry the garlic until crispy and golden brown (adding the tofu/beancurd halfway through, if you didn't bake it). Add the ginger and cook for a further minute. Now add the tofu/beancurd (if you baked it) and sambol olek, stock, tamarind, lime juice, lime leaves, soy sauce and salt.

Stir well, then add the bamboo shoots. Bring to a simmer and cook for 4–5 minutes, then add the beansprouts. Bring back to a simmer and add two-thirds of the basil leaves, roughly torn, stirring them into the broth. Remove from the heat.

Divide the curry into small deep bowls (or transfer into one large serving bowl), and scatter with the remaining basil. Serve with lime wedges and pickled sliced chilli(es)/chile(s) on the side, if you like. I serve this with jasmine or sticky rice.

Right: Thai stilted house, hidden amidst the forest and coconut groves, Ko Pha Ngan, Gulf of Thailand.

STIR-FRIED FERN TIPS WITH PORCINI 'PORK'

300 g/10½. fern tips/fiddleheads, or use 150 g/5¼ oz. asparagus spears and 150 g/5¼ oz. green/French beans
35 g/1¼ oz. dried porcini mushrooms, soaked in boiling water for 15 minutes, or use dried shiitake mushrooms, soaked in boiling water for 15 minutes, or fresh oyster mushrooms
½ tablespoon culinary/unflavoured coconut oil, or use good-quality vegetable oil (see page 13)
4 fat garlic cloves, thinly sliced

MARINADE
2 teaspoons cornflour/cornstarch
1 teaspoon soy sauce, or use tamari or coconut aminos for gluten-free
½ teaspoon date syrup, or use pure maple syrup or coconut sugar
¼ teaspoon salt

SAUCE
2 tablespoons Shaoxing wine, or use dry sherry
1 tablespoon soy sauce, or use tamari or coconut aminos for gluten-free
1 teaspoon ground white pepper

SERVES 3–4

The fact is fern tips, also known as fiddleheads, are not going to be available all year round. You have about a two- or three-week window for your foraging in early spring, as they must only be picked and eaten just after they sprout and start to furl. But it's well worth the effort, as these tender and tasty little shoots have a delicate asparagus-like flavour. You could substitute with asparagus and green/French beans.

This dish is popular across north-east Thailand and Laos, and is usually made with minced/ground pork. It's a super-simple stir-fry that deserves to have a vegan version. You can simply omit the mushrooms if you prefer, or mix it up with some green/French beans. If you do get out for some springtime foraging, some wild garlic also makes a delicious addition.

Blanch the fern tips in boiling water for 30 seconds, then drain in a colander and set aside.

Drain the mushrooms, if using dried, taking care to leave any gritty bits in the liquid (preserve the liquid to use as stock). Finely slice the mushrooms into strips. Mix together the marinade ingredients in a bowl with 2 teaspoons water, and add the sliced mushrooms. Mix well and set aside.

Place a wok or frying pan/skillet over high heat, and add half the coconut oil. Add the mushroom pieces to the pan, and fry for a few minutes whilst stirring. Remove from the pan and drain on paper towels.

Return the pan to the heat, add the remaining oil, and add the fern tips (or whatever substitute you are using) and garlic slices. Stir-fry over high heat for 2 minutes until the garlic is just browning, then add the Shaoxing wine, soy sauce and ground white pepper. Add 1 tablespoon water if the pan is too dry. Mix well, then add the mushroom pieces. Stir-fry for another minute then serve immediately with sticky black rice.

KHAO SEN
Tomato-braised rice noodles with porcini

1½ tablespoons culinary/unflavoured
   coconut oil, or use good-quality
   vegetable oil (see page 13)
1 small brown onion, finely chopped
25 g/1 oz. dried porcini mushrooms,
   soaked in boiling water for
   20–30 minutes, or use other
   wild mushrooms
120 g/4 oz. chestnut/cremini
   mushrooms, roughly chopped
6 fat garlic cloves, finely chopped,
   or use 2 tablespoons garlic paste
8 small red chillies/chiles, chopped
1 tablespoon brown miso paste,
   or use Korean fermented soya bean/
   soybean paste (doenjang)
60 cherry tomatoes (about 700 g/1½
   lb.), or use 2 x 400-g/14-oz. cans
   cherry tomatoes
500 ml/2 cups vegetable stock
1½ teaspoons salt, or to taste
1 tablespoon dark soy sauce,
   or substitute tamari or coconut
   aminos for gluten-free
360 g/12½ oz. vermicelli/rice thread
   noodles

TO SERVE
handful of coriander/cilantro
handful of mint
2–3 spring onions/scallions, thinly
   sliced
1 tablespoon dried chilli flakes/
   hot red pepper flakes
8 bird's-eye chillies/chiles, deep-fried
   (optional)
lime wedges

SERVES 4

It took 18 hours over two days to reach Mae Hong Son, a trip which included three local buses and a 9-hour 'song-thaew' (or share taxi) with 22 people and a broken-down motorbike. We followed the Burmese border snaking around the edge of north-west Thailand. Things appeared a little tense when we arrived at the bus station, with well-armed border police sitting about in trucks and patrolling the local streets. Despite being the only visible 'farangs', we were of no interest to them, and we proceeded to seek out some street food.

I saw this dish bubbling away at the street-food café next door to the one we actually ate in (vegetarian staple of bus station rice). They were serving just this one dish and the broth was deeply meaty, but as I watched the simple construction of a bowl that looked and smelt incredible, I made a mental note. It was almost a decade later when I came across it again and found out just how beloved this dish is in Mae Hong Son. The dish reminds me of an Italian wild boar ragù, and porcini mushrooms make a great substitute for the pork. But that's definitely where the comparison ends. This dish is all about the toppings, which can be adjusted to balance the heat, sourness and saltiness to your own taste.

Add the coconut oil to a wok or large pan and place over medium heat. Add the onion and sauté for 3–4 minutes until softened and translucent.

Drain the soaking mushrooms, taking care to let the gritty bits sink to the bottom, and reserving the strained soaking water for later. Roughly chop the porcini mushrooms, then add the porcini and chestnut/cremini mushrooms to the pan along with the garlic, chillies/chiles and miso. Fry for 2–3 minutes, then add the cherry tomatoes. Bring the mixture to a simmer and cook for 7–8 minutes until the tomatoes are breaking down.

Add the vegetable stock, strained porcini stock, salt and dark soy sauce. Mix well, bring to a simmer again and cook gently for 20 minutes. Taste and add more salt or water if needed.

Soak the noodles in boiling water for 6–7 minutes until softened, then drain well in a colander. Place the noodles in a large bowl and pour over the broth. Mix well, then divide the noodles between the bowls. Scatter each bowl with herbs, sliced spring onions/scallions and dried chilli flakes/hot red pepper flakes. Top with a couple of deep-fried bird's-eye chillies/chiles, if you like, and serve with lime wedges on the side.

PARADISE 'BOUNTY' BARS

Everyone needs a sweeter treat from time to time, and these little bars are the perfect tea break treat! I had been fasting for eight days (yes, you read that right) at an idyllic retreat in a hidden bay on Ko Pha Ngan. I would gaze for hours at their raw dessert counter whilst I was fasting. The vegan bounty bars were usually the first to get snapped up. I was very happy to find how easy they are to make at home.

Do not shake the can of coconut milk. Remove the can lid and, using a spoon, remove 120 ml/½ cup of the thickest part, leaving the watery part behind (you can use this for other dishes).

Place all the ingredients except the chocolate into a food processor or blender and blitz until well combined and slightly smoother.

Place the mixture onto a clean work surface, and shape into eight small bars. Place onto the lined baking sheet, cover and place in the fridge to set for at least 1 hour.

Place a small heatproof bowl over a small pan of simmering water. Add the chocolate to the bowl and let it melt gently. Carefully dip the bottom of the coconut bars into the chocolate, shaking to remove any excess, then place them back onto the baking sheet. Pour the remaining melted chocolate over the bars to create a smooth finish. Sprinkle each bar with a little extra coconut.

Return the coated bars to the fridge for another hour to set completely. The bars will keep in a covered container in the fridge for up to 1 week.

400-ml/14-oz. can coconut milk
100 g/1⅓ cups coarse desiccated/dried unsweetened shredded coconut, plus extra to decorate
50 g/¼ cup coconut yogurt
1 tablespoon date syrup, or use pure maple syrup or coconut sugar
¼ teaspoon vanilla bean paste, or use ½ teaspoon vanilla extract or ¼ scraped vanilla pod/bean
½ tablespoon extra-virgin coconut oil, melted
large pinch of salt
120 g/4 oz. dark/bittersweet vegan chocolate, at least 70% cocoa, broken into pieces

baking sheet, lined with parchment

MAKES 8

Above: Vendor cutting a young green coconut to drink.

SAGO PEARLS WITH PANDAN, BANANA & COCONUT

50 g/⅓ cup small pearl tapioca
    (about 3 mm/⅛ in. diameter)
400-ml/14-oz. can coconut milk
2 tablespoons date syrup, or use pure
    maple syrup or coconut sugar
1 teaspoon vanilla bean paste, or use
    2 teaspoons vanilla extract or
    ½ scraped vanilla pod/bean
large pinch of salt
1 teaspoon pandan paste (see below)
2 ripe bananas, sliced, to serve
2 tablespoons toasted unsweetened
    coconut flakes or shreds, to serve

PANDAN PASTE (MAKES 4 TEASPOONS)
15–20 strips (¼ packet) pandan leaves

SERVES 4

This comforting classic is easy to prepare, and keeps in the fridge up to a week for a dessert treat anytime. It is like a South-East Asian bananas and custard! Good-quality pandan paste is notoriously difficult to find, and extracts rarely contain much of the genuine ingredient and are filled with all kinds of nasties, artificial flavourings and food colourings. It is far easier and cheaper to make your own pandan paste. You can easily freeze the leftovers to use in another dish, savoury or sweet.

Prepare the pandan paste the day before. Chop or cut the leaves into 5-cm/2-in. strips and place in a blender or food processor along with 250 ml/1 cup water. Blend until smooth, then pour into a jar or glass, cover and leave undisturbed overnight.

In the morning, the paste will have separated to the bottom of the glass. Carefully pour out the discoloured water, leaving the thick green paste at the bottom. This can only be done in one movement. If you need to straighten the jar before most of the water has been poured away, set it aside again for a few hours until it separates again, then pour off the remaining water. It doesn't matter if a little water remains in the jar with the paste. The remaining paste can be kept in the fridge for a few days, or freeze to use at a later date.

Place 1.5 litres/6 cups of water in a small pan and bring to the boil over high heat. Add the tapioca and mix well to ensure it doesn't clump. Reduce the heat and simmer gently for about 10–15 minutes until the pearls are translucent. They are cooked even if they still have a small white dot in the centre. Drain the pearls in a sieve/strainer, then rinse well under a cold tap.

In a small pan, heat the coconut milk, date syrup, vanilla, salt and pandan paste. Bring to a gentle simmer, then remove from the heat. Add the tapioca pearls and mix well. Pour the mixture into a container with a lid and leave to cool slightly, before placing in the fridge for a few hours until completely cooled.

When ready to serve, remove the pudding from the fridge and mix well. Divide half the banana slices between four dessert glasses to create a layer on the bottom. Divide half the sago pudding between the four glasses to create an even layer, then top with another layer of banana using the remaining banana slices, and a final layer of sago using the remaining sago. Sprinkle with toasted coconut and serve immediately.

Laos

I would return to Laos in a heartbeat. Our month long trip was mostly dreamy, occasionally interspersed with some parenting challenges. So I have to admit I've often thought about returning there child-free. We mostly explored the northern regions with their misty limestone mountains and ethereal karsts, reminiscent of Khao Sok in southern Thailand. We spent a few weeks travelling up river from Luang Prabang, staying in sleepy villages where the children played petanque with their new local friends, and our hiking was both beautiful and revelatory. The Indo-China war is somewhat absent from the UK high school curriculum. We learnt much from our guides about unexploded ordinance and carpet bombing; exploring caves where the Luang Prabang Phapet Lao army hid out, where there's a giant crater outside as a result of an 800lb bomb that dropped there. At one point, there were 3000 people sheltering inside the darksome cave system with its inner arterial tunnels, bamboo ladders and sub-caves, including the bank and hospital services.

We spent a few days puttering up the glass-like Nam Ou river in our wooden canoe-like boat, between the densely forested mountains, eagerly scouring the skies for hornbills and the river banks for signs of Asiatic bears, or maybe even a tiger! After a few weeks, we looped back down on a public boat towards Luang Prabang, and we made the decision to exit Laos back into Thailand via the border capital of Vientiane, rather than travel the southern route into Cambodia. Partly due to the seriously oppressive heat (which was making our son feel quite unwell), partly due to our soon-to-expire visas and partly because, after more than seven months of travel, the children had truly hit a travel wall that made our full-time travel parenting quite challenging at this point. It wasn't an easy decision to forfeit our planned route to Phonsoram and the Plain of Jars (an iron-age burial site), but we wanted to prioritize the children's needs for some stability, familiarity and air-conditioning. So we spent the next few days contemplating whether to rent a serviced apartment in Bangkok for a week or even a house in the cooler southern parts of Malaysia for a month.

The Buddhist lunar new year celebrations of Pii Mai Laos definitely relieved some of the pressure. This water festival signifies the washing away of the old and the renewal of what's to come; polishing Luang Prabang's temples, Buddhist statues and murals, and the actual self, with daily soakings from the crowds of people who line the streets dousing each other and everyone around them from their water cannons, guns and plastic bottles. Hoses running into giant barrels for refilling the endless showers. There's also cooking pot tar as black as oil, plus bright pink and blue pastes and flour, all liberally thrown or wiped onto cheeks and foreheads. All this water certainly cooled off the children's tantrums. Every main street and side soi is alive and throbbing with happy faces and sloshing water. On New Year's Day the main procession involves a huge papier-mâché water buffalo with giant testicles, and people in traditional costumes trundling down the main street, followed by the immense crowd that slowly crawls its way to Wat Xieng Thoy, also known as the Golden City Temple, to continue the ritualistic cleansing.

As well as much religious ritual in and around the many temples, the days would start with lines of people giving alms to the monks in their varying shades of yellow, orange and saffron. Then the streets would clear and fill with all manner of stalls and many more eating opportunities than usual.

Lots of simple but delicious vegetable dishes, pancakes stuffed with veg and beansprouts and some much needed protein, when we found an Indian street café run by a lovely man from Pondicherry who made us all some spicy tofu/beancurd masala. There had been a distinct lack of protein whilst we'd been in Laos. As a primarily subsistence country, choosing not to eat meat was a definite luxury and we found ourselves relying on salted broad/fava beans, peanut butter and imported French cream cheese, amidst the roasted veg, rice and noodles. After beautiful Luang Prabang and the peaceful riverside villages, we were appalled by the chaotic nature of tourism in Vang Vieng, and then disappointed a little further by orderly and somewhat charmless Vientiane, which just seemed to lack any real charisma. So we made a faster decision than intended to cross the Thai border into Nong Khiaw, which warmly reminded us of Phitsanulok, and we stayed along the banks of the Mekong for a few nights, watching sunrises back over Laos on the other side and wondering when we might ever get to return.

Clockwise from top left: Street view, Luang Prabang; Jungle waterwheel, Kuang Si Waterfalls; Tuk tuk, Luang Prabang; Buddha statue, Wat Si Saket temple, Vientiane.

COURGETTE/ ZUCCHINI & PEACH SOM TAM

8–12 red bird's-eye chillies/chiles, thinly sliced, to taste, or use ½–2 teaspoons chilli/chili paste, to taste

3 fat garlic cloves, or use 1 tablespoon garlic paste

3 courgettes/zucchini

1 small carrot, peeled

small handful of green/French beans, cut into 2.5-cm/1-in. pieces

1½ tablespoons vegan fish sauce (see page 13), or use 1 teaspoon brown miso paste or 1 tablespoon soy sauce, tamari or coconut aminos for gluten-free

¼ teaspoon salt

1½ tablespoons soy sauce, or use tamari or coconut aminos for gluten-free

freshly squeezed juice of 1 lime

1 tablespoon date syrup, or use pure maple syrup or coconut sugar

1 peach, stoned/pitted and cut into 1-cm/½-in. pieces

70g/½ cup unsalted peanuts or cashew nuts, soaked for 1 hour, drained and lightly toasted

handful of coriander/cilantro

SERVES 4 AS A SIDE DISH

Move over Caesar, som tam might possibly be the king of salads! And with dedicated som tam restaurants popping up in bigger cities, this humble dish has been raised beyond its street-food origins. There's a place in Bangkok, buried between the market sois of Sukhumvit (and fortunately only a short walk in the searing heat from the air-conditioned MRT stop), whose Laos-inspired menu, with both traditional and modern influences, celebrates many interpretations of this salad. I've enjoyed so many mouth-popping moments perched on my stool by the window, typically over-ordering when I've been alone. The high stools give a great view of the place, including the open kitchens, where pok pok pok sounds emanate from the dedicated kitchen pounding som tam.

The fact is, green papaya is almost as expensive as beef when it is flown across the planet to be enjoyed in northern Europe. Whilst we can buy fresh papaya grown in Spain and the Canary islands, I have never seen it for sale when it is young, green and crunchy (and som tam-ready). So I started to play around with alternatives like courgette/zucchini, and fruits, such as peach, instead of cherry tomatoes. Stone fruits like peaches are rich in vitamin A, C, E and K, as well as potassium and antioxidants.

Grind the chillies/chiles and garlic with a large pestle and mortar to make a paste, then set aside in a medium–large bowl. If you don't have a pestle and mortar, you can also use a large plastic or metal bowl and grind and pound with the back of a large wooden spoon or rolling pin. It's a bit messy, but effective. If you've touched the chillies/chiles, remember to wash your hands.

Top and tail the courgettes/zucchini, then, using a spiralizer or mandoline, prepare long 'julienne' strips of the courgette, like courgetti/zoodles. Prepare the carrot in the same way or thickly grate it. Add the green/French beans to the mortar and lightly bash to break them down slightly, then add the courgette/zucchini and carrot strips, and pound lightly for another minute to slightly soften the raw veg. Courgette/zucchini is not as robust as green papaya, so be careful not to crush it to a mushy texture.

Add the vegetables to the bowl of chilli/chile and garlic. Add the vegan fish sauce, salt, soy sauce, lime juice and date syrup, and mix well. Finally, add the peach, nuts and coriander/cilantro. Leave to stand for a few minutes, then taste and adjust the sugar or salt accordingly. It should be super spicy, tempered by sweet, sour and salty. You can enjoy the salad immediately, or it'll keep in the fridge for 1–2 days.

ISAN VEGETABLES

30 g/1 oz. dried TVP mince, plus
   2 teaspoons vegetable stock powder/
   bouillon or 1 generous teaspoon
   yeast extract, or use 80 g/3 oz. fresh/
   frozen vegan mince
1 tablespoon rice powder
½ tablespoon culinary/unflavoured
   coconut oil, or use good-quality
   vegetable oil (see page 13)
2 vegan sausages, cut into 2.5-cm/1-in.
   pieces, or use 120 g/4 oz. tofu/
   beancurd, cut into 5-cm/2-in. batons
freshly squeezed juice of ½ lemon
1 small carrot, peeled and sliced into
   5-cm/2-in. batons
1 small brown onion, cut into 2.5-cm/
   1-in. pieces
80 g/3 oz. green/French beans,
   trimmed and halved
100 g/3½ oz. broccoli, cut into small
   2.5-cm/1-in. florets
½ lemongrass stick, very finely chopped
4 fresh or dried kaffir lime leaves,
   very finely chopped
small handful of freshly chopped
   coriander/cilantro, to serve
lime wedges, to serve

SAUCE
1 teaspoon hot chilli/chili paste or sauce
½ tablespoon soy sauce, or use tamari
   or coconut aminos for gluten-free
1 teaspoon date syrup, or use pure
   maple syrup or coconut sugar
½ tablespoon dark soy sauce, or use
   soy sauce or tamari
freshly squeezed juice of ½ lime

SERVES 2–3

Isan people are an ethnic group originating from the Korat Plateau, which sits between Laos, Cambodia and north-east Thailand. Whilst the inhabitants in this north-east region of Thailand are Thai nationals, eighty per cent of the area's population are ethnically Lao, which is reflected in their language and food. Isan food is well known for its spicy chillies/chiles (think mouth-numbing laab/laap), pungent condiments (jaew) and unusual proteins (frogs, snakes, insects and a lot of offal). The Isan fish sauce bplah rah is thicker and funkier than the lighter Thai-style nahm plah. The curries and soups are often clear broths rather than coconut-based, and Isan cooks like to barbeque/grill and roast their produce. Not just meat and fish, but also vegetables and even eggs. This common char-grilling technique imparts so much flavour and seriously raises the vegetable food game.

This dish is common in Laos and north-east Thailand, and you can use whatever seasonal vegetables you have. The roasted rice powder gives a nutty, sticky texture to this fragrant dish. Whilst the sausage is optional, they play a key role in Isan cooking, where you often see these fat little fermented sausages, sour and spicy, sizzling away on the char-grill at street-food stalls. Best served with sticky rice and jaew for an authentic Isan dinner. Recipe pictured on page 115.

Add the dried TVP mince to a bowl, cover with boiling water and add the stock or yeast extract. Mix well and leave to soak for 20–30 minutes. Alternatively, use vegan mince.

Place a large wok over medium heat. Add the rice powder and gently toast until lightly browning. Set aside in small bowl.

Drain the TVP and retain the soaking liquid.

Add the oil to the pan and add the sausage pieces, drained TVP (or vegan mince) and lemon juice. Cook for 6–7 minutes until the sausages are starting to brown on all sides. Now add all the vegetables, the lemongrass and kaffir lime leaves. Turn up the heat to high and stir-fry for 2–3 minutes, until the vegetables start to soften.

Add all the sauce ingredients, the TVP soaking stock and 1–2 tablespoons cold water (or 125 ml/½ cup water if using mince), the roasted rice powder, then mix well so everything is well coated in the sauce. Sprinkle with coriander/cilantro and serve with lime wedges on the side.

VEGAN JAEW BONG
Laos-style roasted chilli/chili sauce

This simple, smoky and spicy condiment is an essential side for any traditional Lao meal. It's very easy to prepare and store, and will keep in the fridge for up to 1 month. It is often served with vegetable crudités for dipping, alongside a cooked vegetable dish, a curry or meat dish and some ubiquitous sticky rice. Recipe pictured on pages 114–115.

1 red onion, quartered
8 fat garlic cloves, or use 2½ tablespoons garlic paste
3–6 long red chillies/chiles, to taste, tops removed
5–7.5-cm/2–3-in. piece of fresh galangal, peeled and thickly sliced, or use ginger
12–18 dried long red chillies/chiles, to taste, soaked in boiling water
4 fresh or dried kaffir lime leaves
2 tablespoons tamarind pulp, or use 1 teaspoon tamarind concentrate plus 2 tablespoons water
2 tablespoons Korean fermented soya bean/soybean paste (doenjang), or use brown or red miso paste
2 tablespoons date syrup, or use pure maple syrup or coconut sugar
1 teaspoon salt, or to taste
½ tablespoon culinary/unflavoured coconut oil, or use good-quality vegetable oil (see page 13)

baking sheet, lined with parchment

MAKES 300 ML/1¼ CUPS

Preheat the oven to 210°C (400°F) Gas 6.

Arrange the onion quarters, garlic cloves, fresh chillies/chiles and galangal (or ginger) on the lined baking sheet. Bake in the preheated oven for 15 minutes until well browned.

Remove from the oven and cool slightly. Place all the roasted ingredients and all the remaining ingredients, except the oil, into a blender. Blitz until fairly smooth.

Add the oil to a small pan or wok, add the paste and stir-fry over medium heat for 6–7 minutes, stirring often, until fragrant. Take care not to burn. Taste and add more salt if needed.

Cool the mixture and store in a sterilized jar for up to 1 month in the fridge.

Left: French colonial building and bicycle in UNESCO World Heritage site Luang Prabang, Northern Laos.

SOUR PUMPKIN & MUSHROOM SOUP

900 ml/scant 4 cups good-quality
    vegetable stock
425-g/15-oz can straw mushrooms,
    rinsed and drained, or use 500 g/
    1 lb. 2 oz. button or torn oyster
    mushrooms (healthiest option)
4 red chillies/chiles, finely chopped
3 fat garlic cloves, finely chopped,
    or use 1 tablespoon garlic paste
2 lemongrass sticks, trimmed,
    bruised and finely chopped
2.5-cm/1-in. thumb of fresh galangal,
    or use ginger, peeled and thinly sliced
4–5 fresh or dried kaffir lime leaves,
    to taste
½ small pumpkin (about 500 g/
    1 lb. 2 oz.), peeled, seeds removed
    and cut into bite-sized chunks,
    or use any squash
freshly squeezed juice of 2–3 limes,
    to taste
1 teaspoon salt
140 g/5 oz. vegan Quorn pieces,
    or use any ready-to-use vegan
    'mock chicken'
2 spring onions/scallions, sliced at
    an angle
small handful of coriander/cilantro

SERVES 4

Cycling is definitely one of the best ways to explore Luang Prabang. The town itself is a revered UNESCO site, so there's much to see biking around the old streets. French and Indo-Chinese architecture, saffron-clad monks receiving alms, sparkling gilded temples, stopping for street food and watching sunsets where the Mekong and Khan rivers meet. We spent several weeks here after the children made some local friends and were reluctant to move on – they enjoyed visiting local homes and joining in religious ceremonies. Then came Pii Mai Laos, the water-soaked Buddhist new year celebrations, which brought welcome relief from the April heat.

This dish typically includes chicken but can easily be made vegan. The sour flavourful broth is contrasted by the sweet pumpkin and nutty mushrooms. I like to add mock chicken pieces at the end for extra protein. In the UK, I use Quorn pieces and in Italy and France, I use soy-based mock chicken. Recipe pictured on page 114.

Add the stock to a large pan, and add the mushrooms, chillies/chiles, garlic, lemongrass, galangal and kaffir lime leaves. Bring to the boil, then reduce the heat to low and simmer for 5 minutes.

Add the pumpkin and continue to simmer until the pieces are just cooked, then add the lime juice, salt and Quorn pieces. Simmer for another 2–3 minutes, then remove from the heat.

Add the spring onions/scallions and coriander/cilantro. Mix well and serve immediately.

SOOP PAK
Warm vegetable salad

5 fat garlic cloves, unpeeled
3 large red chillies/chiles, tops removed
2.5-cm/1-in. thumb of fresh ginger, peeled and thinly sliced
2 tablespoons soy sauce, or use tamari or coconut aminos for gluten-free
45 g/⅓ cup sesame seeds, mixture of white and black ideally
½ Chinese cabbage, cut into 5–7.5-cm/2–3-in. pieces
¼ cauliflower, cut into bite-sized florets
140 g/4½ oz. bamboo shoots, drained and rinsed
large handful of green/French beans, trimmed and halved
250–300 g/9–10½ oz. collard or spring greens, or use pak choi/bok choy
4 oyster mushrooms, torn into strips
handful of freshly chopped coriander/ cilantro
2 stems of dill, roughly chopped

baking sheet, lined with parchment

SERVES 4

The streets of Luang Prabang are a haven of Lao street food. Stall after stall, with Ottolenghi-style cooked salads piled high, surrounded by a few benches or plastic chairs, perfect for people-watching whilst enjoying your food. The vegetable combinations seem to be endless, and the stall holders will bag up any combos for a ready-made picnic.

A Lao soop is prepared as a cooked vegetable salad or thick, herby stew. You can use a variety of vegetables, depending on the season and what you have in the fridge. The key element to this dish is the toasted sesame seeds. I prefer to make this dish the day before and allow it to reach room temperature before serving with sticky rice. Recipe pictured on page 114.

Preheat the oven to 190°C (375°F) Gas 5.

Place the garlic and chillies/chiles onto the lined baking sheet and roast in the preheated oven for 10–15 minutes until deep golden brown. Remove and leave to cool. Peel the garlic, and remove any burnt skin on the chillies/chiles, then add the garlic and chillies/chiles to a blender or food processor with the ginger and soy sauce, and blitz to a paste. Set aside.

Place a frying pan/skillet over medium–high heat, add the sesame seeds and toast until they become fragrant and the white seeds start to colour. Remove from the heat and let cool slightly. Place the seeds in a mortar and grind to rough paste using the pestle. You can also use a spice grinder to do this.

Place all the vegetables into a steamer, and cook for 8–10 minutes until tender. Drain and set aside to cool.

Place the cooked vegetables into a large bowl and add the chopped herbs, roasted paste and ground sesame seeds. Using your hands, mix well until everything is well coated. The salad will keep in the fridge for 1–2 days. Serve at room temperature.

SAKOO YAT SAI
Tapioca dumplings with tofu/beancurd & cashews

225 g/1½ cups small pearl tapioca (about 3 mm/⅛ in. diameter)
large pinch of salt
175 ml/¾ cup hot, almost boiling, water

FILLING
1 teaspoon toasted sesame oil, or use good-quality vegetable oil (see page 13)
½ small brown onion, finely chopped
3 fat garlic cloves, finely chopped, or use 1 tablespoon garlic paste
4 coriander/cilantro stems, chopped
80 g/3 oz. firm tofu/beancurd, crumbled
2 small red chillies/chiles, finely chopped
2 spring onions/scallions, sliced
2 tablespoons vegan fish sauce (see page 13), or use soy sauce or tamari
1 teaspoon ground white pepper
3 tablespoons cashew nuts, lightly toasted and roughly chopped

TO SERVE
½ cucumber, deseeded and sliced into 5–7.5-cm/2–3-in. batons
1 carrot, peeled and sliced into 5–7.5-cm/2–3-in. batons
125 g/4 oz. mooli/daikon radish, peeled and sliced into 5–7.5-cm/2–3-in. batons
2 sticks of celery, trimmed, peeled and sliced into 5–7.5-cm/2–3-in. batons
vegan jaew bong (see page 113), for dipping
soy sauce, for dipping, or use tamari for gluten-free

MAKES 12

These substantial dumplings are a popular street food across Laos and Thailand, most likely influenced by Chinese cooking. It's hard to find ones with vegan fillings, so it's worth having a go at making some at home. They can be a little time-consuming to prepare, but are actually quite easy to put together. Naturally gluten-free, these make a great starter, or can be served alongside other dishes as part of a small banquet. The prepped dumplings can also be frozen before they are cooked, then popped in a steamer when needed. Dense, chewy and filling, serve them with raw vegetables and vegan jaew bong (see page 113) dipping sauce on the side.

To prepare the dough, start by placing the tapioca pearls in a small bowl with the salt. Add the hot water and mix together quickly with a spoon. The mixture will quickly form a stiff dough. Cover with a damp cloth and set aside for 20 minutes.

For the filling, place a small frying pan/skillet over medium heat and add the sesame oil. Add the onion and sauté for about 4–5 minutes until translucent, then add the garlic and coriander/cilantro stems. Cook for another 1–2 minutes, then add all the remaining filling ingredients except the nuts. Cook for about 4–5 minutes until everything is aromatic and well combined. Remove from the heat and add the nuts. Mix well and set aside.

To prepare the dumplings, using wet hands, divide the tapioca dough into 12 small balls, plus one spare ball. Take one ball and press a small hole with your thumb into the top to create a little cup. Add 1–2 teaspoons of the filling mixture, then fold up the edges and fill the hole with a small piece of dough from the spare ball, if needed. Smooth the ball with wet hands to seal well. Set on a sheet of parchment and cover with a damp cloth. Repeat to make 12 dumplings in total.

Place a large bamboo or other steamer over a pan of boiling water, with a small piece of parchment to partially cover the bottom. Place the dumplings into the steamer and cook for 30 minutes until translucent and sticky.

Serve immediately with vegetable crudités, jaew bong and soy sauce or tamari for dipping.

STICKY BLACK RICE CAKES WITH COCONUT & PEACHES

These little Laos-style pudding parcels are traditionally made using banana, but you can use whatever soft, sweet fruit is in season, such as nectarines, mangoes, apricots and plums. You can also use baking parchment, but banana leaves impart a sweet, earthy flavour to the dish, and there is something lovely about unwrapping your own dessert. Any leftovers are lunchbox-ready.

The peach-coconut continuum is often used as an analogy to explain cross-cultural communication styles. 'Peach' cultures are considered 'softer', and more open to making new friends (such as South Americans) whereas 'coconut' cultures are seen as harder on the outside and less open to newcomers (such as Northern Europeans). My husband calls this peach version 'yin yang farang' (farang is the Thai/Lao word for foreigner), because the component parts are quite different to each other. But it turns out that peach and coconut are very happy bedfellows.

250 g/1 cup black glutinous/sticky rice, soaked overnight in cold water, or use white glutinous (sweet) rice
200 ml/scant 1 cup good-quality coconut milk
4 tablespoons coconut sugar
¼ teaspoon salt
½ tablespoon good-quality vegetable oil (see page 13)
2 ripe peaches, stoned/pitted and each cut into 8 thick slices, or use canned
4 pieces of banana leaf, cut into 20 x 30-cm/8 x 12-in. rectangles
4–5 tablespoons coconut cream, to serve

MAKES 4

Drain and rinse the soaked rice, then place in a small pan with the coconut milk, sugar and salt. Bring to a simmer and cook for 5–6 minutes over low heat until the coconut milk has been absorbed. Remove from the heat and add the oil. Mix well and set aside to cool.

Wipe the banana leaves with a damp, warm, clean cloth, which will also help soften them slightly (you can also soak in water or microwave for a few seconds). Place one banana leaf rectangle on the work surface, and place 1 heaped tablespoon of the cooled rice in the centre. Arrange 4 peach slices on top of the rice (half a peach), then another tablespoon of rice. Fold the sides of the leaf over, wrapping it like a snug parcel. You shouldn't need to secure with string/twine if the banana leaf is well softened. Repeat with the remaining leaves, rice and peaches.

Place a large pan or wok, quarter-filled with water, over high heat. Bring to the boil, then place a steamer over the water and carefully place the rice parcels, seam-side down, into the basket. Cover and steam for 45–50 minutes. Serve warm with a drizzle of coconut cream, if you like.

Vietnam

Our previous trips to South-East Asia had barely touched Vietnam, after spending a lengthy stretch in Laos on an extended visa during our gap year. We found ourselves heading back to Bangkok for a stint of modernism (specifically requested by our 7-year-old twins – an actual sofa to sit on whilst watching Star TV), as our son had been a little unwell. Nothing serious, but we had been propelled into a travel wall.

We were travelling overland at the time, and had taken a less-travelled northern route through Laos to the Vietnam border. Just after the new year celebrations of Pii Mai Laos in April, it had been hot and dry in the northern regions for months. The travel wall often hits when you've been on the road for a while and overwhelming homesickness and a deep yearning for familiarity follows you around. It never lasts though. And our trusted formula of a city apartment, home-cooked food and air conditioning was just the week everyone needed.

Fast-forward 15 years and me reaching 50, I decided it was time to take a trip that was less backpacker and even more bucket list than usual. I had always wanted to take the train from north to south Vietnam on the reunification railway. We had an idea to do this, as cheaply as possible, during our backpacker days, but this time I was hoping for some comfort. We arranged to meet the twins in Hanoi, once they had finished their work and studies for the Christmas holidays. Lee and I arrived a few days early, after a month exploring lesser known corners of north-east Thailand.

We spent a week exploring Hanoi, then up to the eastern region and a surprise trip to Ha Long Bay. Eager to do some sun-seeking after a rather chilly and rainy time in the north, we followed the coast south by train, stopping in Da Nang then the ancient port town of Hoi An.

Hoi An sits a little inland, along the banks of the Thu Bon river and connected by bridges to the small islands/eyots that form the broken-up land across the broad river mouth. Some of the delta areas are flooded and used for rice growing, but others are well populated, such as Cam Nam, one of the larger delta islands connected by bridges to the old town and the areas north of the river. Here, we found a charming homestay with bicycles, and a matriarch who was very happy to cook for us.

Early one morning, we donned our sun hats and headed north of the village. A chance to explore the old town on bikes, before anyone else is awake, then further north, riding well-kept pathways amongst the vast paddy fields, intersected by the occasional modern road. We stopped for bags of fresh fruit and coconut, took the long way around an intersection to avoid a large angry snake that had found itself stuck on a central reservation, and eventually found a nice stretch of beach close to Ao Nang. It had been a long time since I'd seen so many backpackers and it made me feel old. But we had fun catching some waves in the surfy water, and enjoyed our sunset ride back through villages and paddy fields.

We explored the many foodie corners of Ho Chi Minh City, which were outstanding for vegans and vegetarians. Finally, we headed out to the island of Phu Quoc to do some research for our Italian retreat, and a little snorkelling and free-diving. We all fell in love with Phu Quoc with its vast sandy beaches, unspoilt forests and friendly villages. Parts of the island are facing serious challenges managing the influx of tourism, and I felt torn between wanting to return and playing a role in the very visible problem. Phu Quoc has an environmental pressure group working to develop more sustainable tourism practices. But there's visibly a long way to go yet.

Clockwise from top left: Old-fashioned rickshaw, Hoi An; 'Dark and Bright' Cave, Lan Ha Bay; florist vendor at market in Hanoi; street market, Hanoi; Buddhist prayer flags and ancient tree, Hanoi.

CA PHE SUA DA
Vietnamese-style iced coconut coffee

Traditionally made, Vietnamese coffee is not particularly healthy as it uses condensed milk, which is packed with sugar (yes, even the vegan versions). My Hanoi-loving friend Urvashi told me to look out for the iced versions, and it was then that I found my new drinking love. You can make a hot version by blending the coconut milk and cream with the dates, then heating gently before straining and adding the coffee. And of course substitute decaffeinated coffee if, like me, you prefer not to spike your adrenal system.

60 ml/¼ cup coconut cream, or use other vegan cream or an additional 60 ml/¼ cup thick coconut milk
2 large pitted dates, roughly chopped
100 ml/generous ⅓ cup coconut milk, thick part only
500 ml/2 cups ice
4 espresso shots of freshly brewed French coffee (about 100 ml/ generous ⅓ cup total)

TO SERVE
cocoa powder, for dusting (optional)
coconut shavings or desiccated/dried unsweetened shredded coconut, lightly toasted (optional)

MAKES 2 LARGE OR 4 SMALL

Add the coconut cream and dates to a blender or food processor and blitz until smooth. Add the thick coconut milk and blitz again until smooth. If you want the mixture to be completely smooth, and without bits, pour it through a fine sieve/strainer.

Add the mixture back to the blender or food processor along with the ice, and blitz until a slushy mixture forms. Pour into a container with a lid and place in the freezer for 30–40 minutes.

Meanwhile, prepare the espresso shots and let them cool in the fridge or freezer. This will stop the slushy melting too quickly.

Remove the slushy mixture from the freezer and divide between two large glasses (or four small), then pour the coffee over the top. Dust with cocoa powder and sprinkle with lightly toasted coconut shavings or desiccated/dried unsweetened shredded coconut, if you like. Serve immediately.

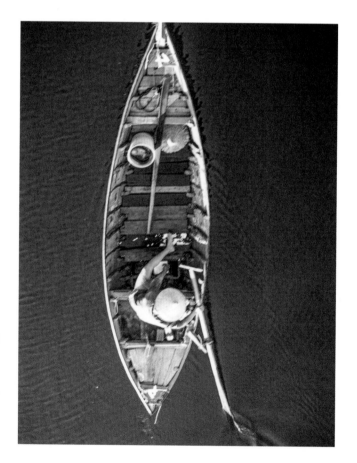

Left: Small fishing boat on Ho River, Cau De Vong bridge, Cam An, Hoi An.

BUN CHA *with smoky tempeh patties*

100 g/3½ oz. vermicelli/rice thread
    noodles
1–2 teaspoons good-quality
    vegetable oil (see page 13)

TEMPEH PATTIES
200 g/7 oz. tempeh, roughly crumbled
½ x 20-cm/8-in. square nori sheet,
    finely chopped
1 tablespoon gram flour (chickpea/
    garbanzo bean flour)
¼ teaspoon ground white pepper
¼ teaspoon dried chilli flakes/
    hot red pepper flakes
1 teaspoon cornflour/cornstarch,
    or use potato starch
½ teaspoon salt

DIPPING SAUCE
1 tablespoon rice vinegar
2 tablespoons date syrup, or use pure
    maple syrup or coconut sugar
1 tablespoon vegan fish sauce
    (see page 13) or soy sauce, tamari
    or coconut aminos
2 small red chillies/chiles, finely
    chopped
1 fat garlic clove, finely chopped,
    or use 1 teaspoon garlic paste
small handful of coriander/cilantro
    stems, finely chopped

SALAD
50 g/¼ cup beansprouts
70g/2½ oz. iceberg lettuce, or use
    romaine leaves or Little Gem/Bibb
small handful of coriander/cilantro
    and mint leaves
85 g/3 oz. cucumber, thinly sliced

SERVES 2

Christmas was just around the corner, and the streets of Hanoi sparkled with lights in every window and doorway. Christmas songs blared from tiny speakers strung under street canopies, where mechanical Santas and penguins in sledges waved their arms. Every few steps along the street took you into a different song, as George Michael and Mariah competed for our attention. From the balcony of our quaint guest house on a tiny street in the old town, the delicious wafts of street food and steaming buns amidst the Christmas-themed cacophony drew us out to explore this fascinating city.

This simple little soup is truly loved in Vietnamese homes and on the street-food stalls of Hanoi. Less well known than pho, bun cha are thin round rice noodles served with broth, griddled meat patties, greens and herbs ('bun' means noodle in Vietnamese). We tried a vegan version at a popular vegan restaurant in Hanoi, where the patties were made with chickpeas/garbanzo beans, which you could substitute if you prefer. My version is super simple to make using flavourful smoky tempeh spiked with nutritious nori.

For the tempeh patties, put the crumbled tempeh into a mixing bowl with all the other patty ingredients and combine well until the mixture comes together. Shape the mixture into 8–10 bite-sized patties. Set aside.

Place the rice noodles in a small pan of boiling water and simmer for 4–5 minutes over medium–high heat. Drain, place in a serving bowl and set aside.

Place a large frying pan/skillet over high heat, add the vegetable oil and fry the patties on each side for 1½ minutes. Remove and place onto paper towels to drain any excess oil.

Mix the dipping sauce ingredients together with 250 ml/1 cup water and add to the serving platter with the noodles. Add the patties and all the salad ingredients. Serve.

COM TAY CAM
Crispy claypot rice

After a few days exploring what felt like every street of Hanoi, heavily fuelled by frequent coffee stops and street-food snacking, we decided to splurge on a trip to Ha Long Bay. This was definitely the stuff of bucket-list dreams, although when we left at dawn in the torrential rain, passing giant mega mall-style buildings, half-constructed holiday apartment blocks and tacky pearl outlets, we started to have our doubts.

Despite being a UNESCO-protected area, Ha Long Bay is still a commercial thoroughfare, as well as saturated with less than responsible tourism. But I had done my homework, and we enjoyed incredible Vietnamese hospitality aboard a beautiful and responsibly managed modern boat, that took us to a less explored area called Lan Ha Bay and Cat Ba Biosphere Reserve. We kayaked our way through magical caves and coves of Tai Keo Island, enjoyed incredible food and even took a cooking lesson with the crew.

Amongst the many salads, noodles and curries, we also enjoyed a variety of claypots, which are heavily influenced by Chinese cooking. This was definitely one of my favourites. Very comforting and warming, with delightful soft and crispy textures. You can substitute the pickled mustard greens for your own quick pickled vegetables (see page 131) if you prefer.

180 g/1 cup jasmine rice
250 ml/1 cup vegetable stock
1 tablespoon culinary/unflavoured coconut oil, or use good-quality vegetable oil (see page 13)
3 fat garlic cloves, finely chopped, or use 1 tablespoon garlic paste
2.5-cm/1-in. thumb of fresh ginger, peeled and finely chopped, or use 1 heaped tablespoon ginger paste
120 g/4 oz. firm tofu/beancurd, cut into 2.5-cm/1-in. thick batons
½ teaspoon five-spice
1 tablespoon soy sauce, or use tamari or coconut aminos for gluten-free
large pinch of ground white pepper
1 tablespoon Shaoxing wine, or substitute dry sherry or rice wine
150 g/5½ oz. assorted fresh mushrooms, such as oyster, king oyster, enoki and shiitake, sliced
1 teaspoon toasted sesame oil
2 small heads of pak choi/bok choy, trimmed and stems separated, or use Chinese lettuce
2 spring onions/scallions, thinly sliced at an angle and separated into white and green parts

SAUCE
1 tablespoon vegan fish sauce (see page 13), or use soy sauce or tamari
½ tablespoon date syrup, or use pure maple syrup or coconut sugar
1½ tablespoons vegan 'oyster' sauce, aka mushroom stir-fry sauce
80 ml/⅓ cup vegetable stock

TO SERVE
2–3 tablespoons pickled mustard greens
chilli/chili oil

SERVES 2

Place the rice in a sieve/strainer and rinse well under a cold tap until the water runs clear. Drain the rice and place in a medium-sized claypot or lidded non-stick pan with the stock. Set aside to soak for 1 hour.

In a wok or frying pan/skillet, add ½ tablespoon of the coconut oil and place over medium–high heat. Add the garlic and ginger, and cook for 1–2 minutes, then add the tofu/beancurd pieces and sprinkle with five-spice. Mix well so the tofu/beancurd pieces are well coated in the spices. Add the soy sauce, pepper and Shaoxing wine. Mix well and stir-fry over medium–high heat until all the liquid has reduced and the tofu/beancurd is starting to caramelize. Place the tofu/beancurd onto a plate and set aside.

Put the claypot or pan with the soaking rice over medium heat and bring to a simmer. Turn the heat down to the lowest setting, cover with the lid and continue to cook the rice slowly until all the water has been absorbed, about 12–15 minutes. Do not stir.

Add the remaining coconut oil and the sliced mushrooms to the pan you cooked the tofu/

beancurd in and stir-fry for 3–4 minutes until just starting to brown, then tip onto the plate along with the tofu/beancurd. Now add ½ teaspoon of the sesame oil and the pak choi/bok choy to the pan and quickly sear until just wilted. Remove from the heat.

Once the rice is just cooked, layer the tofu/beancurd, sliced mushrooms and pak choi/bok choy on top of the rice and scatter with the white parts of the spring onions/scallions. Mix all the sauce ingredients together in a small bowl, then pour over the dish. Maintaining the low heat, cover the claypot or pan. Cook gently for a further 15–20 minutes. Halfway through the cooking time, drizzle the remaining ½ teaspoon sesame oil around the edges of the pan to help the rice get crispy.

When cooked, scatter with the spring onion/scallion greens and serve with pickled mustard greens and chilli/chili oil on the side.

Above: Ha Long Bay junk boats.

STUFFED BANANA LEAVES *with pickled vegetables*

We rolled into Da Nang on an overnight train from Hanoi. We had ordered train food delivered to our private family cabin, but it was honestly some of the worst food we had ever eaten on a train. Da Nang appeared to be as sleepy and bleary-eyed as we felt, so we headed over to the nearest street café to investigate their plant-based offerings. As ever, a simple noodle soup with crunchy veggies and spicy, sour and sweet condiments on the side, plus an ice-cold pineapple shake, hit the spot we were seeking. After agreeing a price with the taxi driver who had been touting us since we left the station, we stuffed our rucksacks as best we could into the boot of his car and set off on the next leg of our adventure.

We were on our way to Hoi An, an ancient fishing port and possibly one of the most tourist-swamped places I've ever visited. We found a charming homestay just over the river from the old town, with plenty of rented bicycles for us to explore the streets and alleyways of this remarkable place. There are very good reasons that, on average, over 4 million tourists visit every year. Hoi An is like stepping back in time – if you de-sensitize yourself to the crowds, avoid the night markets at peak time and mostly avoid any of the eateries sitting along the river front. Again, simply terrible tourist food.

But it wasn't all like that thank goodness. We sought out the bakery made famous by Anthony Bourdain, and queued for an hour to experience their vegan take on a banh mi (and we arrived there early!). I'd also heard about some of the fantastic vegan restaurants on the other side of town. After a couple of fabulous meals, we decided to pick up some food to travel with for the next leg of the journey – including these steamed and stuffed banana leaves. Making for a much healthier and more satisfying wait at the airport. Recipe pictured on page 132.

6–8 large pieces of banana leaf (about 35 x 25 cm/14 x 10 in.)
375 g/1½ cups glutinous/sticky rice, soaked overnight in cold water

FILLING
6 fresh or dried shiitake mushrooms, or use dried porcini
1 tablespoon culinary/unflavoured coconut oil, or use good-quality vegetable oil (see page 13)
3 fat garlic cloves, finely chopped, or use 3 teaspoons garlic paste
1 aubergine/eggplant, cut into 2-cm/¾-in. pieces, or use 2 small courgettes/zucchini
1 small carrot, peeled and cut into 6-mm/¼-in. pieces
½ sweet potato, peeled and cut into 1-cm/½-in. cubes
small handful of green/French beans, fresh or frozen, trimmed and cut into 2.5-cm/1-in. pieces
2 tablespoons soy sauce, or use tamari or coconut aminos for gluten-free
1 generous tablespoon brown miso paste
1 tablespoon date syrup, or use pure maple syrup or coconut sugar
1 teaspoon sesame oil
1 teaspoon tamarind pulp, or use ¼ teaspoon tamarind concentrate, or substitute with rice vinegar
½–1 teaspoon salt, to taste
2 spring onions/scallions, thinly sliced
handful of freshly torn coriander/ cilantro

**PICKLED VEGETABLES
(MAKES 250 ML/1 CUP)**

2 carrots, peeled and sliced into
    julienne strips
1 mooli/daikon radish, peeled and
    sliced into julienne strips
2 teaspoons sugar (any)
1 teaspoon salt
3–4 tablespoons date syrup, or use
    pure maple syrup or coconut sugar
250 ml/1 cup rice vinegar
175 ml/¾ cup warm water

TO SERVE
sambol olek or hot chilli/chili sauce
    (optional)

MAKES 6–8

Start by making the filling. If using dried mushrooms, soak them in boiling water for 15–20 minutes. Remove once softened, then squeeze out the excess water. (Keep the soaking water, if you like, for adding to vegetable stock in another recipe.) Roughly chop the mushrooms and set aside.

Place a large pan or wok over high heat, add the coconut oil and the garlic. Cook gently until the garlic is slightly crispy, then add the mushrooms and all the other filling ingredients, except the spring onions/scallions and coriander/cilantro. Cook for 15 minutes until everything is starting to soften and combine. Remove from the heat and stir in the spring onions/scallions and coriander/cilantro.

Wipe the banana leaves with a damp, warm, clean cloth, which will also help soften them slightly (you can also soak them in water or microwave for a few seconds). Rinse and drain the soaked rice.

Take one of the banana leaf rectangles and add 2 tablespoons of the uncooked soaked rice to one side of the rectangle, leaving 5 cm/2 in. space at the outside edge (it is easiest to make this the edge closest to you with the rectangle pointing away). Then add 3 heaped tablespoons of the filling mixture on top of the rice. Top with another 2 tablespoons of rice and another spoonful of vegetables.

Now carefully fold over the edge closest to you and start to roll over the parcel, trying not to squash it too much. Once rolled two-thirds of the way up the rectangle, fold in the two sides of the leaf together, tucking in the edges as if wrapping a parcel – pushing any filling back inside that has started to reach the edges. Once these sides are well tucked, roll over the last part of the leaf, which should self-seal if the leaves are well softened. Set aside, with the seam facing down. Repeat for the remaining banana leaves, rice and filling.

If you need to, you can tie them with a piece of string/twine, like a traditional gift wrapping! You can also use parchment for this, instead of banana leaves. (It is easier to wrap using parchment, since you can cut to a large size, but make sure you double up the layers if using parchment.)

Place a large steamer or adjustable steamer basket over a large wide pan, with 5 cm/2 in. water in the bottom. If using a metal steaming basket that sits in the bottom of a pan, you will also need the pan lid. Bring to the boil and then place the parcels carefully in the steamer. Simmer over low heat for 1½–2 hours until the rice is fully cooked.

To make the pickled vegetables, add the julienned vegetables to a bowl and add the sugar and salt. Massage well using your hands, so all the vegetables are well coated. After a few minutes, the vegetables will become more flexible, so the strips do not snap when bent. Place the vegetables in a colander and rinse well with cold water. Drain and add to a large bowl. Add the date syrup, vinegar and warm water. Mix well and then set aside.

Serve the parcels unwrapped with a side of the pickled vegetables, and sambol olek or hot chilli/chili sauce, if you like.

COM GA HOI AN
Vietnamese chick'n rice

1 tablespoon olive oil
¾ teaspoon salt, plus extra to taste
½ teaspoon ground turmeric
360 g/2 cups basmati rice, or use any other long-grain rice
1 tablespoon Korean fermented soya bean/soybean paste (doenjang), or use brown or red miso paste
freshly squeezed juice of 2 limes (about 4–5 tablespoons)
1 tablespoon date syrup, or use pure maple syrup or coconut sugar
1 small brown onion, thinly sliced
¼ teaspoon ground white pepper, plus extra to taste
½ tablespoon good-quality vegetable bouillon or stock powder
5-cm/2-in. thumb of fresh ginger, peeled and thinly sliced
180 g/6 oz. tofu/beancurd skins, twists/knots or small sticks
2 handfuls of Vietnamese mint, roughly torn, or use 1 small handful of coriander/cilantro and 1 small handful of mint, plus a little lemon balm or lemon zest

TO SERVE

3-4 bird's-eye or small red chillies/chiles, thinly sliced
3-4 tablespoons soy sauce, or use tamari or coconut aminos for gluten-free
3-4 teaspoons white miso paste
900 ml/4 cups hot water, just off the boil
2 spring onions/scallions, thinly sliced at an angle, separated into whites and greens

SERVES 4

There is an upside to a town like Hoi An having such a high influx of tourists... and that's the ease of finding really great vegan restaurants serving local takes on classic dishes. I've envied the 'chicken rice' dishes across South-East Asia for decades. We were biking around town in the early morning, enjoying the relative quiet, avoiding street food carts piled high with tiny baguettes, when I spotted a vegan restaurant I had been reading about. Traditional Vietnamese cooking, but vegan. This kind of find used to be the holy grail whilst travelling, a decade or two ago. Although Hoi An boasts several great vegan places, this one was the star. So I made a mental note of the location, and we returned that night.

When I tried their vegan version of Vietnamese chicken rice or com ga, I realised what all the chicken and rice fuss was about. And that we should get to enjoy a meat-free version. Tofu/beancurd skin is a great foil for faking chicken texture, and using umami-rich stock to cook the rice together with the fresh herbs and tangy lime, makes for a very comforting dish. Vietnamese coriander/cilantro is an essential ingredient and can be found in Asian stores. Slightly spicy and lemony, it's sometimes called hot mint. You can use a combination of coriander/cilantro, mint leaves and even lemon balm if you have, it or Thai basil as a substitution. When lemon balm isn't in season, I use a little sprinkle of lemon zest along with the herbs. Recipe pictured on page 133.

Prepare the rice first. Place a heavy-bottomed, lidded pan over medium–high heat and add the olive oil, ¼ teaspoon salt and the ground turmeric. Add the rice and sauté for 2 minutes, mixing well so the rice is evenly coated. Transfer to a rice cooker, if you prefer to use one. Add 500 ml/2 cups water and the Korean soya bean/soybean paste. Mix well and switch the rice cooker to cook, or, if using a lidded pan, bring to a simmer. Cook gently for 10–12 minutes until the rice is 90 per cent cooked and the water is absorbed (adding a little more water if needed). Remove from the heat, cover with a clean kitchen towel and the pan lid on top, then set aside for 10–15 minutes to steam gently.

Add the juice of 1 lime and ½ tablespoon date syrup to a medium bowl, and 60 ml/¼ cup water and the thinly sliced onion. Mix well and set aside for 10–15 minutes.

To prepare the dressing, add the juice of the remaining lime, the remaining ½ tablespoon date syrup, ½ teaspoon salt and the white pepper to a small bowl and mix well. Set aside.

Add 400 ml/1¾ cups water to a small pan, along with the veg bouillon or stock powder and ginger. Place over high heat and bring to a simmer. Add the tofu/beancurd skins, reduce the heat and simmer for 3–4 minutes. Remove from the heat and set aside to cool, leaving the tofu/beancurd skins in the stock mixture.

Once cooled, remove the tofu/beancurd skin pieces and lay on a plate. Using your hands or a sharp knife, roughly tear or chop the skins to make bite-sized shredded pieces. Place in a medium–large bowl, along with the dressing and the drained onion slices. Mix well. Add the roughly torn herbs and a little more salt and white pepper to taste, mixing everything well.

To serve, put the thinly sliced chillies/chiles into a small bowl with the soy sauce and mix well. Combine the white miso with the slightly off the boil hot water to make a light soup. Pour into four small serving bowls or cups, and sprinkle with some spring onion/scallion greens.

Fluff the cooked rice, then layer onto a large bowl or plate. Top the rice with the 'chicken' mixture, sprinkle with the remaining spring onions/scallions and serve immediately with the soy and chilli dressing and a cup of miso soup on the side.

Above: Riverside fishing village,
Ho River, Cam An, Hoi An.

VIETNAMESE-STYLE RICE CRACKERS *with sesame & chia*

A healthy twist on a simple and naturally healthy rice cracker, usually sun-dried but an oven will suffice. These baked and crunchy little beauties are protein-packed with nutritious sesame and chia seeds, and incredibly easy to make. Once cooked, they can be stored in an airtight container for several weeks. A delicious, crispy accompaniment for lots of South-East Asian dishes and curries. Recipe pictured on page 133.

50 g/scant ⅓ cup cooked white rice
2 tablespoons toasted sesame oil
1 teaspoon fine salt
100 g/scant 1 cup glutinous (sweet) rice flour, or use tapioca flour/starch
1 level tablespoon chia seeds
1½ teaspoons black sesame seeds
1½ teaspoons white sesame seeds

baking sheet, lined with parchment

MAKES 8

Above: Bustling street, Ho Chi Minh City. Right: Fishing boats on Duong Dong River, Phu Quoc island.

Preheat the oven to 190°C (375°F) Gas 5.

Add the cooked rice, oil, salt and 75 ml/⅓ cup water to a food processor or blender, and blitz until smooth. Pour the mixture into a small bowl and add the flour and seeds. Use your hands to mix and combine well to form a dough, which will be fairly dry and breakable. Use your hand to squeeze the mixture together to form a ball (add a little more water if needed), then cover and set aside for 20–30 minutes to rest.

Cut two squares of parchment, approximately 15 cm/ 6 in. wide. Divide the dough into eight balls, kneading the dough to press the mixture back together.

Place a ball of dough on the parchment and press down with your hand to flatten it slightly. Cover with the other sheet of parchment and roll gently with a rolling pin, turning the parchment with each roll, to create a large, thin piece of dough, 3 mm/⅛ in. thick. You can use your fingers to smooth out any cracks near the edges, by rubbing on top of the parchment.

Peel off the top sheet and then carefully transfer the thin piece of dough onto the lined baking sheet. Repeat until you have filled the sheet, then place in the preheated oven for 8–10 minutes until crispy.

Once cooled, the crackers will keep for several weeks in an airtight container.

MONK'S PLATTER
Simple tofu/beancurd curry & bamboo shoot salad

Phu Quoc is the largest island in Vietnam and sits on the edge of the Cambodian border, sharing the eastern waters in the Gulf of Thailand and a passion for pepper growing. The island has a long history of tourism, as well as being home to one of the most famous fish sauces in South-East Asia.

We spent blissful days filled with scooting, beachcombing (and rubbish collecting), yoga, snorkelling and exploring the many varied aspects of this beautiful, but rapidly developing, island. This paradise lost has unfortunately been found by large investment companies who are building on a scale that is often mismatched to the beauty of the landscape. Vast holiday resorts and casinos are springing up on formerly pristine coastline. Although it was the giant cable car, reportedly the longest across the sea in the world, and the huge swathes of development eating into the National Park areas that had me wondering how the protected status of this island is being upheld.

We ate in numerous street-food markets and cafés around the local villages, including the main town of Duong Dong, where the former airport runway (now a free-for-all road) transforms into a market haven at night. I asked our taxi driver about the route we would have taken before the new airport was constructed. He said, exactly the same route. Down the runway, between take-offs and landings!

This Monk's Platter, with small bowls of simple Vietnamese-style tofu/beancurd curry, crunchy salad, soy dressing and sticky rice, was a popular go-to vegan offering on general menus.

SIMPLE TOFU/BEANCURD CURRY

½ tablespoon culinary/unflavoured coconut oil, or use good-quality vegetable oil (see page 13)

1 tablespoon curry powder

2–3 lemongrass sticks, trimmed and bruised

280 g/10 oz. firm tofu/beancurd, cut into 2.5-cm/1-in. cubes

200 g/7 oz. taro, peeled and cut into 2-cm/¾-in. cubes

1 small–medium aubergine/eggplant, cut into 2-cm/¾-in. cubes

120 g/4 oz. green/French beans, trimmed and halved

7–8 fresh or dried curry leaves, to taste

1 teaspoon salt

1 teaspoon good-quality vegetable stock powder or bouillon

1 tablespoon date syrup, or use pure maple syrup or coconut sugar

200 ml/scant 1 cup coconut milk

freshly squeezed juice of 1 lime

SALAD

freshly squeezed juice of 1 lime

1 teaspoon rice vinegar

1 teaspoon date syrup, or use pure maple syrup or coconut sugar

¼ teaspoon salt

120 g/4 oz. canned bamboo shoot sticks, rinsed and drained, or use fresh, peeled and cut into 2.5-cm/ 1-in. batons

1 carrot, peeled and sliced into julienne strips or grated

¼ cucumber, deseeded and cut into 2.5–5-cm/1–2-in. batons

2 tablespoons peanuts, lightly toasted

SIDE DRESSING

3 tablespoons soy sauce, or use tamari or coconut aminos for gluten-free

1 spring onion/scallion, thinly sliced

TO SERVE

handful of Vietnamese mint, roughly torn, or use Thai basil and mint

sticky black rice

SERVES 2–3

Start by making the curry. Place a large wok or deep frying pan/skillet over medium heat and add the oil and curry powder. Turn down the heat to low and cook the powder until fragrant, about 30–40 seconds. Add the bruised lemongrass sticks and stir-fry for another 1–2 minutes.

Add the tofu/beancurd, taro and aubergine/eggplant, and mix well so the pieces are well coated in spices. Stir-fry everything for another 4–5 minutes. Add 500 ml/2 cups cold water to the pan, and turn up the heat. Bring to a simmer and add the remaining curry ingredients except the lime juice, then gently simmer for another 5–7 minutes until all the vegetables are tender. Add the lime juice just before serving.

For the salad, mix together the lime juice, rice vinegar, date syrup and salt in a small bowl. If using fresh bamboo shoot, blanch in boiling water for 5 minutes, then drain. Add the salad vegetables and peanuts, and mix well.

For the side dressing, mix the soy sauce and spring onions/scallions in a small bowl.

To serve, lay a small mound of sticky black rice, on a large plate for each diner, with two small bowls and a dipping bowl. Fill one bowl with some curry and the other with salad, and add a little dipping sauce to the dipping bowl. Scatter a few fresh herbs onto the curry and salad.

BANH TRANG NUONG
Rice paper pizza

It took two attempts to try a veggie version of this deliciously crunchy street food classic at a night market. The first time, my poor efforts at explaining I didn't eat meat failed and the trader was far from friendly about it. But then we were shoulder-to-shoulder in a tourist-packed Hoi An night market. I had already been reprimanded for taking a photograph of someone's paper lanterns, so realised pretty quickly that the tourist-weary traders were fed up with being stared at like some kind of exhibit, and ashamedly put my camera away, embarrassed by my own insensitivity. I can't imagine what it's like for the older villagers witnessing the transformation of their home. Imagine if half the population of London chose to visit Colchester during one year!

One evening we set off to explore the night markets long after we had eaten earlier at a fantastic vegan eatery west of the old town. It was quite late, so some traders had already begun to pack up for the night, hoping there would be slightly fewer Instagrammers. I was happy just to wander, as the options for veggie and vegan street food beyond roasted corn cobs hadn't been extensive so far. Then I spotted a trader making rice-paper pizzas. As I approached and my smile was returned, I pointed to the ham and explained I didn't eat that bit. His smile broadened and he starting to concoct a veggie version in a matter of seconds. The small barbeque/grill was perched atop a large old drum, and he lay the unsoaked rice paper onto the grill. Working quickly he drizzled, smeared, scattered and drizzled some more before folding the crispy taco-like shell with one swift crunch. One-handed street food really lives up to its name. Although don't tell my Italian friends, who think walking and eating is a slight abomination.

3 scant tablespoons gram flour (chickpea/garbanzo bean flour)
1 scant teaspoon ground turmeric
¼ teaspoon black salt
4 rice paper sheets
3 spring onions/scallions, green part only, thinly sliced
3–4 heaped tablespoons vegan cream cheese, such as Bute Island Scheese
4 slices Vietnamese vegan 'chicken ham', sliced into small strips, or use any vegan ham or bacon (optional)
2 small red chillies/chiles, finely chopped
2 tablespoons crispy shallots (see page 82, but use shallots instead of onions and garlic, optional)
2 tablespoons vegan mayo, to serve
2 tablespoons siracha, or any chilli/chili sauce, to serve

MAKES 4

Place a large frying pan/skillet over high heat. In a small bowl, whisk the gram flour, ground turmeric and black salt with 6 tablespoons water until a smooth batter forms.

Lay one rice paper sheet onto the hot pan, and toast for 30 seconds. Turn down the heat to medium and smear the rice paper with a tablespoon of the gram flour batter, making sure it forms a thin layer that almost reaches the edges but doesn't spill over. Sprinkle the top with the spring onion/scallion greens, then add small blobs of vegan cream cheese and scatter the vegan ham (if using) across the 'pizza'.

Turn the heat down to medium–low, if browning too quickly, and cook for another few minutes until the toppings are melting and the underside is starting to brown. Scatter with chillies/chiles and crispy shallots, if using. Drizzle the mayo and chilli/chili sauce across the top in a large zigzag pattern, so there is an even distribution of sauce.

Carefully fold the rice paper in half. It will crack a little – but try to do it in one gentle but swift action, folding like a quesadilla. Toast gently for another 20–30 seconds, turning once.

Repeat with each rice paper sheet. Eat immediately!

BANH KHOT
Turmeric crispy pancakes with marinated tempeh

The twins were flying home from Ho Chi Minh City, so I spent hours researching the best way to spend their last day in Vietnam (not least because we were staying on for longer). I made a hit-list of history, culture, food and more food to explore. Ho Chi Minh City is home to vibrant and expansive markets, serving some of the city's greatest street food.

Top of my list was the cavernous Binh Tay market, and the neighbouring streets that are packed with street cafés and food carts. Binh Tay is one of the largest markets in the city, situated in the heart of Chinatown. It has an almost-department-store layout with balconied upper floors overlooking the thousands of densely packed stalls below, with triple the content of every conceivable item. The piled-high stock creates narrow alleyways with produce spilling into every corner. It seemed like everything you could ever need would be found in this market somewhere. At the rear of the market, there's also a huge food court serving authentic street food, albeit a little challenging when you're looking for something plant-based.

Ben Thanh market is one of the oldest market sites in Ho Chi Minh City, dating back to the 17th century. The original structure has endured the ravages of colonial rule and a decade-long war. In the early morning, it's a hive of activity in the huge vaulted halls, selling everything from fresh and dried produce to clothing and engine parts. It later turns into a bustling night market. Just across from this old site, is the trendy Ben Thanh street-food market, a more recent addition serving traditional dishes and more accessible vegan options, mainly aimed at tourists and local hipsters.

When I spotted the banh knot pan in one of the narrow alleys, I peered over to get a glimpse of the filling. There was meat, seafood and even tofu, so I took my place in the reassuring queue. Best served lettuce wrapped, with the crispy little shell giving an explosion of fresh flavours with a gooey, savoury centre. There are specific banh knot pans, but you can easily use a mini muffin pan, or even better a Japanese Takoyaki pan, as the rounded shape makes the perfect mini cup shape. This shortened recipe uses cooked rice instead of soaked mung beans in the batter.

Left: Ben Thanh street food market, Ho Chi Minh City.

225 ml/scant 1 cup coconut milk

70 g/½ cup leftover cooked rice

85 g/⅔ cup rice flour

40 g/⅓ cup glutinous (sweet) rice flour,
or use tapioca or cornflour/
cornstarch

1 teaspoon ground turmeric

1 teaspoon salt

225 ml/scant 1 cup sparkling water

2–3 spring onions/scallions, sliced and
separated into white and green parts

4 tablespoons extra-virgin coconut oil,
or use good-quality vegetable
oil (see page 13)

FILLING

120 g/4 oz. tempeh, cut into
2 x 3-cm/¾ x 1¼-in. pieces

1 fat garlic clove, finely chopped,
or use 1 teaspoon garlic paste

½ teaspoon ground white pepper

1 tablespoon soy sauce, or use tamari
or coconut aminos for gluten-free

1 teaspoon date syrup, or use pure
maple syrup or coconut sugar

TOPPING

4 tablespoons coconut cream,
or use thick coconut milk

2 teaspoons tapioca starch

pinch of salt

TO SERVE

6–7 romaine lettuce leaves, trimmed
and cut into 7.5-cm/3-in. squares,
or use iceberg

small handful of freshly torn mint,
coriander/cilantro and basil

pickled vegetables (see page 131)

nuoc mam dipping sauce (see page
145), or use ready-made sweet chilli/
chili or siracha sauce

banh khot pan, mini muffin pan
or takoyaki pan

MAKES 20–24

To make the batter, put the coconut milk and cooked rice in a blender or food processor, and blitz until smooth. Add the rice flours, turmeric and salt to a large bowl, and mix well. Add the coconut and rice mixture, and sparkling water. Whisk until smooth, then add the spring onions/scallions, keeping back a spoonful of the greens to garnish. Mix everything until well combined. Leave to stand for at least 1 hour in the fridge.

Place the filling ingredients into a bowl and mix well. Set aside.

Add a scant ¼ teaspoon of coconut oil to each of the muffin pan holes, or brush the pan holes generously with oil. Place the pan over high heat for a minute or two. If using a muffin pan, place the pan on a cast-iron hot plate. Heat until smoking hot.

Pour a generous tablespoon of batter into each hole, and allow to bubble slightly for 30 seconds, turn down the flame to medium if using a banh knot or takoyaki pan (maintain high heat for muffin pan on cast-iron plate). If using a muffin pan, tip the pan in different directions to cover the sides of the holes a little, which will create a crispy little basket shape. Add a marinated tempeh piece or two into the centre of each. Fry gently for 1–2 minutes until starting to crisp on the outside.

Drizzle each pancake with a little more batter, approx. 2 teaspoons. Cover the pan (you will need to use foil if using a muffin pan). Cook for a further 2–3 minutes. Remove the lid or foil and cook for a further minute to ensure the outside shell is nice and crispy. Remove the pancakes from the pan and place on paper towels to drain excess oil. Transfer to a baking sheet and keep warm in a low oven while you cook the rest of the batter. These little pancakes can also be cooled and reheated later in a medium oven, although the centre will be less gooey the longer they spend in the oven.

To make the creamy topping, add the coconut cream and tapioca starch to a small pan. Whisk until well combined and smooth, then heat gently over low–medium heat until gently simmering and thickened. Add a pinch of salt.

Place each pancake onto a little lettuce square. Pour a half teaspoon of the creamy coconut topping into each pancake, and scatter with assorted herbs. Serve immediately with pickled vegetables and nuoc mam dipping sauce on the side.

NUOC MAM
Vietnamese-style dipping sauce

This ubiquitous little dipping sauce is usually made with Vietnam's much-beloved fish sauce. This vegan version is super quick to prepare and will keep in the fridge for several weeks. It can be served on the side of banh knot, banh cuon, summer rolls and fritters. Recipe pictured on page 143.

Below: Fruit for sale. Street vendor with bicycle, Hanoi Old Town.

4 tablespoons vegan fish sauce
  (see page 13)
50 g/⅓ cup coconut sugar
3 fat garlic cloves, finely chopped,
  or use 1 tablespoon garlic paste
1–2 small red chillies/chiles, to taste,
  thinly sliced
1 tablespoon rice vinegar
freshly squeezed juice of 1 lime

MAKES 250 ML/1 CUP

Add the vegan fish sauce, coconut sugar and 150 ml/⅔ cup water to a small pan. Bring to a simmer and cook until the sugar has dissolved. Turn off the heat and set aside to cool slightly.

Combine all the remaining ingredients in a small bowl, add the mixture from the pan and mix well. Set aside for 20–30 minutes until completely cooled and ready to serve.

BANH CUON
Shiitake-stuffed steamed rice pancakes

120 g/1 cup rice flour
120 g/1 cup tapioca flour
1 teaspoon salt
1 tablespoon culinary/unflavoured coconut oil, melted, or use good-quality vegetable oil (see page 13), plus extra for greasing

FILLING
45 g/1½ oz. (about 7–8) dried shiitake mushrooms, soaked in boiling water for 15 minutes
1 teaspoon sesame oil
100 g/3½ oz. mooli/daikon radish, peeled and cut into 3-mm/⅛-in. dice
3 spring onions/scallions, thinly sliced, white parts only
1 fat garlic clove, finely chopped, or use 1 teaspoon garlic paste
½ tablespoon vegan 'oyster' sauce, aka mushroom stir-fry sauce
1 teaspoon soy sauce, or use tamari or coconut aminos for gluten-free
¼ teaspoon white pepper

TO SERVE
shredded lettuce, such as iceberg, Little Gem/Bibb or romaine
¼ cucumber, deseeded and sliced into 5-cm/2-in. thin batons
small handful of mint
small handful of coriander/cilantro
small handful of beansprouts
2 tablespoons pickled vegetables (see page 131)
1 tablespoon crispy shallots (see page 82, but use shallots instead of onions and garlic, optional)
nuoc mam (see page 145)

MAKES 4–5

These rice pancakes are much easier to make than you might think. And when you make them at home, you can fill them with all sorts of combinations of your favourite things to eat. For a super-fast, tangy snack, simply roll the pancake and drizzle in your favourite sauces, such as nut butter, soy and chilli/chili, and top with fresh herbs, nuts and seeds. Like any pancake making, be prepared to let the first one look a lot shabbier than the last one. The more you make, the better you'll become at making them thin and soft, but slightly thicker versions are equally delicious. Patience is key. This healthful recipe has an umami-rich filling, and is topped with crunchy pickles and fragrant herbs.

Mix the rice flour, tapioca flour, salt and 1 litre/4 cups room temperature water in a bowl, whisking until well blended. Add the oil and whisk until combined. Let rest for 15 minutes.

Carefully drain the shiitake mushrooms, gently squeezing out any excess water (retain for other recipes). Roughly chop.

Place a wok or frying pan/skillet over medium–high heat and add the sesame oil. Add the mushrooms and mooli/daikon, stir-frying for 2 minutes. Stir in the spring onion/scallion whites and the garlic. Reduce the heat to medium–low and cook for 3 minutes. Stir in the 'oyster' sauce, soy sauce and white pepper. Let cool.

Place a lidded frying pan/skillet over low heat (I find it easiest to make the pancakes in a 20–25 cm/8–10 in. pan). Wipe the pan surface with oil, coating sparingly. Do the same to a large plate.

Pour approximately 180 ml/¾ cup of the batter into the pan – the amount may depend on the size of your pan.

Place the lid on the frying pan/skillet and cook for 1–2 minutes until the pancake starts to become translucent and almost cooked through. Remove the pan lid. Add 1–2 tablespoons of filling along the lower centre of the pancake, then roll up gently using a spatula, still in the pan. Transfer to a plate by simply sliding the roll onto the plate (the rolls are very sticky and break easily). Repeat with the remaining pancake batter and filling.

To serve, scatter the top of the pancakes with shredded lettuce, cucumber batons, herbs, beansprouts, pickled vegetables and crispy shallots, if using. Serve with a bowl of nuoc mam on the side. You can also drizzle the pancakes with hoi sin sauce and/or siracha for a more street-food tourist vibe, if you like, but bear in mind that these ready-made sauces are very high in sugar.

COCONUT BANH GAN *with strawberry star anise sauce*

200 ml/scant 1 cup coconut milk
3 tablespoons coconut sugar,
   or use white sugar for no colouring
1 tablespoon cornflour/cornstarch,
   plus 1 tablespoon water, to make
   a paste
¾ teaspoon agar powder
1 teaspoon vanilla bean paste,
   or use ½ scraped vanilla pod/bean
   or 2 teaspoons pure vanilla extract
350 g/1¾ cups live Greek-style
   coconut yogurt

SAUCE
300 g/10½ oz. fresh or frozen
   strawberries, tops removed and
   halved, plus extra fresh sliced
   strawberries to serve (optional)
2 tablespoons coconut sugar,
   or use unrefined brown sugar
small pinch of salt
1 star anise, seeds removed and
   crushed

*4 small, deep soufflé-style pots,
lightly oiled*

SERVES 4

I served banh gan on my street-food menu for several years before developing this vegan version for our retreat menu. This dessert uses our annual glut of strawberries, sublimely paired with star anise. Using coconut sugar will impart a slight caramel colour, or use white sugar if you prefer to keep it looking white.

Prepare the sauce by placing a small pan over low heat. Add the strawberries, sugar, salt and star anise. Gently simmer for 15–20 minutes until the fruit breaks down completely and reduces to a thick sauce. Remove from the heat and allow to cool slightly. Pour the sauce into a fine sieve/strainer, and push through using a spatula, so that the seeds are all removed and the sauce is clear and smooth. Set aside for later.

Place the oiled pots in a deep baking tray/sheetpan. Wipe off any excess oil using paper towels.

Add the coconut milk and sugar to a small pan and place over low heat. Add the cornflour/cornstarch paste, agar powder/flakes and vanilla, whisking the mixture all the time to ensure there are no lumps, and everything is well combined and smooth. Cook gently until thickened, about 4–5 minutes, continuously whisking. Allow then mixture to cool a little (so it doesn't destroy the good bacteria in the yogurt), then add the yogurt and whisk really well to ensure the mixture is very smooth and well combined. You can use a blender at this stage, to make this mixture as smooth and silky as possible.

Divide the mixture between the pots and place in the fridge to cool and set for at least 1 hour. When ready to serve, allow to come to room temperature for 30 minutes. Turn out onto small plates, then drizzle with strawberry sauce. Serve immediately with extra sliced strawberries, if you like.

PETIT POTS DE CREME COCO
French-style chilli/chili chocolate pots with raspberry & mint

70 g/2½ oz. dark/bittersweet vegan
  chocolate
½ tablespoon extra-virgin coconut oil
25 g/¼ cup unsweetened cocoa powder
¼ teaspoon chilli/chili powder (this
  gives a gentle end kick – increase
  to ½ teaspoon for less subtle heat)
2 tablespoons date syrup, or use pure
  maple syrup or coconut sugar
250 ml/1 cup coconut milk, thickest
  part only
2 teaspoons coconut sugar
140 g/1 cup fresh or frozen raspberries,
  plus extra fresh raspberries to
  decorate (optional)
12 mint leaves (optional)

4–6 small glass pots

MAKES 4 LARGE OR 6 SMALL

I learned to make the classic version of these pots when I was 10, after browsing through my mum's 70s cookbook. It was my first attempt at a grown-up dessert, and they came out perfectly. I even served up a hazelnut version to Michel Roux Jr. in a MasterChef heat. In recent years, I've been making a vegan version using coconut cream and the best of Italian chocolate. Until our recent trip, I had no idea that Vietnam produced such incredibly good-quality chocolate (and coffee), and we enjoyed visiting some of the many chocolatiers in Hanoi. This fusion dessert is perfect for a South-East Asian dinner party finale.

Melt the chocolate and oil in a small heatproof bowl set over a pan of simmering water.

Sift the cocoa and chilli/chili powder into a large bowl, add the date syrup and thick coconut milk, whisking until well combined and smooth. Whisk the mixture for 3–4 minutes to make it light and fluffy – using a hand-held electric mixer will give much lighter results. Finally, add the melted chocolate and whisk again until smooth and well combined.

Divide the mixture between four or six small glass pots and chill in the fridge for 30 minutes.

Place the coconut sugar and raspberries in a small pan and bring to a simmer over medium–low heat. Cook gently for 3–4 minutes until all the fruit is broken down. Pour the sauce through a sieve/strainer to remove all the seeds. Set aside to cool.

Divide the cooled raspberry sauce between the choc pots, covering the puddings with a thick layer of raspberry sauce. Cover and chill the pots in the fridge until needed. Allow the pots to come to room temperature for a couple of hours before serving (or they will be too firm) and decorate with a couple of fresh mint leaves and extra fresh raspberries, if you like.

MALAYSIA & INDONESIA

Malaysia

On our first trip to South-East Asia, Lee and I barely trod on Malaysian soil as we passed through so quickly on our way to Sumatra. A few station snacks and a couple of nights in Penang gave us a little taste, but it wasn't until after the children were born that we spent more time there.

During our gap year we took a road trip around the peninsula, stopping to explore the coast and the country's numerous islands. We zigzagged across the country to get lost in the beautiful Cameron Highlands, where we picked strawberries and enjoyed the freshest of tea with scones after our lengthy hikes. And if I can, I will always try to grab a few days of outstanding eating in Kuala Lumpur.

More recently, just before the twins were heading off to university, we took a month-long trip down through Thailand's west coast, taking what felt like a refrigerated bus into Northern Malaysia from Hat Yai. Instead of the usual route across to Butterworth and Penang, I had been reading about a National Marine Park called Pulau Payer. There seemed to be little information about the islands, other than they were supposedly pristine and uninhabited. On paper, it looked like we could travel to the Kedah region and, from the main port town, we might be able to take a boat out to visit them. We arrived into the city of Alor Setar very late at night and exhausted from a bus journey that had started at 6am. It became clear fairly quickly that we'd arrived somewhere unused to seeing tourists and we found ourselves the subject of much staring as we tried to find a place to stay in town. Eventually we were directed to a very tall and shiny-looking hotel, adjacent to a giant Tesco Lotus hypermarket. Much to our delight, one half of this giant car park turned into a bustling street food market at night. Stools were set around low tables, the sounds and smells of sizzling roti canai, curries and barbeques filled the atmosphere, and families and children noisily filled the space. This was everyone's favourite place to eat. Sadly there were no boats. They stopped years ago the woman at the port office informed me. The only people who visit those islands, she said, are day trippers from package resorts in Langkawi and Penang. Whilst Alor Setar wouldn't be at the top of my Malaysian destination recommendations, we spent our few days there exploring the bustling city, visiting traditional Kedahan Malay houses and museums, and returning to the beloved foodie car park at night.

We eventually reached Penang a few days later, and after a few more enquiries, we found a boat that took trips to the elusive islands. The woman at the port wasn't wrong about the day trippers, and whilst the islands are extraordinarily beautiful, they are somewhat overrun and the currents are dangerously strong. But we did get to snorkel with sharks on New Year's Day, and whilst the boat food was extraordinarily bad, we also got to spend another week in much loved Penang, staying in Georgetown, a truly gourmet epicentre for vegetarians and vegans in Malaysia.

Clockwise from top left: Malaysian architecture, Penang; Fields of tea, Cameron Highlands, Peninsular Malaysia; Cycle rickshaw, Georgetown, Penang; Street-food stall, Melaka; Traditional Colonial house, Georgetown, Penang.

CHAR KOAY KAK
Savoury turnip cake stir-fry

This popular dish originated in China, but has its own unique version in Malaysia and Singapore, where its cubed and stir-fried with soy, beansprouts and chilli/chile. You'll find this smoky stir-fry in any Malaysian hawker food court, and at street food stalls and hawker stands in Chinatowns across South-East Asia. The name may sound slightly confusing, because it's actually made from the Asian radish known as mooli/daikon. But turnips are a little similar to mooli/daikon, with a slightly milder flavour. And mooli/daikon is distinctly different to the hot and peppery European radish. So it actually makes sense that this is called turnip cake. It gets more confusing in Singapore, where it can be referred to as carrot cake.

Hawkers take a prepared chunk of cake, and chop it onto the sizzling hot steel, adding sauces, beansprouts and greens, and sometimes stir-fry it with an egg. It is then served on a tray with some more crunchy toppings and chopsticks. Chai poh is preserved radish that has a salty, sweet and funky crunch. Easily found in Chinese stores, along with other preserved pickled veg, such as mustard greens.

The radish cake can be cut into squares or rectangles, and served simply stir-fried with dipping sauces like soy, sambol olek and black vinegar (lo bak gou). This street-food-style recipe uses stir-fried pieces and spikes up the savoury (and healthful) with shiitake mushrooms and stir-fried greens to make a satisfying light meal.

1 mooli/daikon radish (550–600 g/ 1 lb.3 oz.–1 lb. 5 oz.), grated
25 g/1 oz. (about 6–8) dried shiitake mushrooms, soaked in 250 ml/ 1 cup boiling water for 20 minutes, or use dried porcini
½ tablespoon culinary/unflavoured coconut oil, or use good-quality vegetable oil (see page 13)
1 banana shallot, finely chopped
2 fat garlic cloves, finely chopped, or use 2 teaspoons garlic paste
¼ teaspoon salt
½ teaspoon ground white pepper
180 g/1½ cups rice flour
1 tablespoon tapioca starch, or use cornflour/cornstarch

BATTER
1 tablespoon gram flour (chickpea/ garbanzo bean flour), plus 3 tablespoons water, well blended
¼ teaspoon black salt
¼ teaspoon ground turmeric

STIR-FRY
½ tablespoon culinary/unflavoured coconut oil, or use good-quality vegetable oil (see page 13)
2 tablespoons chai poh (preserved radish), or use preserved mustard greens (optional)
2 teaspoons vegan fish sauce (see page 13), or use soy sauce
2 tablespoons vegan oyster sauce, aka mushroom stir-fry sauce, or use hoisin sauce
large handful of beansprouts
2 heads of pak choi/bok choy, or use chard, leaves separated and roughly torn
4 spring onions/scallions, thinly sliced at an angle and separated into white and green parts
½ teaspoon salt

TO SERVE

small handful of beansprouts

small handful of freshly torn coriander/
 cilantro

sriracha, or use other chilli/chili sauce

standard loaf pan or 12.5–15-cm/
5–6-in. square baking pan (about
5 cm/2 in. deep), lined with parchment

SERVES 4–5

Place the grated mooli/daikon in a pan and add enough water to just cover. Place over medium heat and simmer gently for 50–60 minutes until the mooli/daikon is more translucent and just cooked. Drain in a colander and leave to cool. Once cool, squeeze out any excess liquid.

Drain the mushrooms (preserving the stock for later use), and roughly chop. Put a small frying pan/skillet over high heat and add the oil. Add the shallot and mushrooms, stir-frying for 3–4 minutes until the shallots are just translucent. Add the garlic and cook for another minute or so, then add the salt and pepper, mixing well. Remove from the heat and set aside.

Add the rice flour and tapioca starch to a large bowl, then add the mixture from the frying pan/skillet and the cooled mooli/daikon. Strain the mushroom soaking water through a fine sieve/strainer to remove any gritty bits, then add more cold water, if needed, to make 200 ml/scant 1 cup. Add this liquid to the bowl and mix to combine everything evenly. The mixture should have the consistency of very thick porridge.

Pour the mixture into the lined pan and smooth the top of the mixture with a spatula or spoon. Place a large, deep bamboo steamer over a pan of boiling water and place the baking pan into the steamer, then cover. If you don't have a bamboo steamer, you can use a large, wide, deep pan, and place a steaming rack inside. Cover the pan with a clean kitchen towel and then cover with a lid. This will reduce the moisture dripping into the cake

during cooking. Steam the cake for 50–60 minutes until it feels firm when you press it gently. The outside layer may still be a little sticky, but this will firm up as it cools. Set aside to cool completely (overnight in the fridge is best).

To serve as a snack or dim sum, simply slice into rectangles and fry for 2–3 minutes on each side until browned and crispy. Serve with dipping sauces.

To prepare the street food-style stir-fry, it is better to make two portions in the wok at a time, using approximately half the cake. Halve the turnip cake, and cut one half into roughly bite-sized pieces with a sharp knife. Different sized pieces create the different bites of chewy and soft and crispy bits, which is the best kind of char koay kak.

Mix together the batter ingredients and set aside.

Place a large wok over high heat and add half the coconut oil, then add the cake pieces, and stir-fry for 4–5 minutes, so that the pieces start to crisp and brown. Use a spatula to press the pieces into the pan to char slightly. Now add half the chai poh, if using, and stir-fry for another 1–2 minutes.

Add half the vegan fish sauce and half the vegan oyster sauce, together with half the beansprouts, half the pak choi/bok choy, half the spring onion/scallion whites and half the salt. Stir-fry over high heat for about 1–2 minutes, mixing well. Pour half the gram flour batter over the mixture, and allow to set slightly before flipping over. It doesn't matter if pieces break up – most street food hawkers chop into the bound pieces of cake to create three or four big pieces.

Set aside cooked pieces in a warm oven, and repeat with the remaining half of the ingredients to prepare another two portions.

Once all the pieces are cooked through, place onto serving plates, and scatter with spring onion/scallion greens, a handful of beansprouts, a handful of coriander/cilantro leaves and a drizzle of hot sauce, if you like.

FASTER LAKSA WITH ZOODLES

250 g/9 oz. firm tofu/beancurd, cut into 2.5-cm/1-in. cubes, or use ready-made tofu/beancurd puffs (these are deep-fried)

2 tablespoons cornflour/cornstarch, or use potato starch

2 tablespoons extra-virgin coconut oil, melted, or use cooking oil spray

3–4 tablespoons red curry paste

1 tablespoon mild curry powder

1 tablespoon Korean fermented soybean paste (doenjang), or use brown or red miso paste

800 ml/scant 3½ cups good-quality vegetable stock

400-ml/14-oz. can coconut milk

1 tablespoon vegan fish sauce (see page 13)

½ tablespoon date syrup, or use pure maple syrup or unrefined coconut sugar

1 tablespoon unsweetened peanut butter, or use almond or cashew (omit date syrup if sweetened)

1 teaspoon salt

160 g/5¾ oz. mock chicken, such as vegan Quorn, or use firm tofu/beancurd

16 vegan fish balls (optional)

2 large courgettes/zucchini

TO SERVE

large handful of beansprouts

2–3 tablespoons sambal balado (see page 197) or sambol olek

small handful of freshly chopped coriander/cilantro

small handful of freshly chopped mint

lime wedges

baking sheet, lined with parchment

SERVES 4

Curry laksa is a staple Malaysian (and Singaporean) dish. This deeply savoury and spicy noodle soup is packed with proteins, but can be a little time-consuming to make from scratch (refer to My Vegan Travels for a more traditional laksa paste recipe).

This recipe is a 'cheat' version that equally delivers on flavour. Ready-made laksa paste can be a little tricky to find, but this version can be made with the more readily available red curry paste. It's crucial to use a good-quality vegetable stock, and you can use rice or yellow noodles, if you prefer. The low-carb trend for making vegetable noodles works brilliantly in this flavourful broth, but it's important to load the healthy fats and protein to create a satisfying bowl of food.

Preheat the oven to 200°C (400°F) Gas 6.

Place the tofu/beancurd pieces in a bowl and add the cornflour/cornstarch. Using your hands, toss the tofu/beancurd pieces so they are well coated, then lay the tofu/beancurd pieces on the lined baking sheet and drizzle with 1 tablespoon of the coconut oil, or spray with oil. Bake in the preheated oven for about 15–20 minutes until just crispy. Transfer to paper towels and set aside. You can omit this stage and use ready-made tofu/beancurd puffs, but bear in mind these are deep-fried.

In a deep frying pan/skillet or wok, add the remaining oil and place over medium–high heat. Add the red curry paste and cook for a few minutes, constantly stirring to cook out the spices. Now add the curry powder and soybean paste. Reduce the heat to medium and cook for a further 2 minutes.

Add the vegetable stock, coconut milk, vegan fish sauce, date syrup, peanut butter and salt. Mix well and bring to a simmer or 5 minutes. Reduce the heat to low and add the baked tofu/beancurd, mock chicken and vegan fish balls, if using. Simmer gently for another 5 minutes.

Top and tail the courgettes/zucchini, and then use a mandoline or spiralizer to slice the courgettes/zucchini into 'courgetti' or 'zoodles' (long, thin, spaghetti-like strips). Place a small pan of boiling water on the stove and blanch the courgetti/zoodles for 60 seconds, then quickly remove and drain in a colander.

Divide the courgetti/zoodles between four bowls, then ladle the broth into each, dividing the tofu/beancurd, fish balls and mock chicken evenly between the dishes. Top with a spoonful of fresh beansprouts and a small spoonful of sambal. Scatter with a few fresh herbs and serve immediately with lime wedges on the side.

SIMPLE MALAYSIAN VEGETABLE CURRY

Malaysian-style curry has a more gentle, sweeter heat, with warm cinnamon and fennel. Like much of Malaysian food, this dish is heavily influenced by South Indian and Sri Lankan cooking. This curry is simple to prepare, and even easier if you replace the spice mixture with a ready-made Malaysian curry spice mix. I like to prepare my own spice blends, not least because there is nothing quite like freshly toasted and ground spices. Once they are packaged for commercial sale and transited, something is lost forever. The best way to save time is to make more spice mix than you need, so next time it becomes a quick dish. Serve with acar awak seasonal vegetable pickle (see page 161). Recipe pictured on page 162.

1½ tablespoons culinary/unflavoured coconut oil, or use refined olive oil or pomace oil
240 g/8½ oz. firm tofu/beancurd, cut into bite-sized pieces
160 g/5¾ oz. okra, cut into 2-cm/ ¾-in. pieces
1 red onion, finely diced
8 fat garlic cloves, finely chopped, or use 2½ tablespoons garlic paste
5-cm/2-in. thumb of fresh ginger, peeled and finely chopped, or use 2 heaped tablespoons ginger paste
4-cm/1½-in. thumb of fresh turmeric, or use 1 teaspoon ground turmeric
1 lemongrass stick, bruised
2 star anise
7.5–10-cm/3–4-in. cinnamon stick
½–1 teaspoon chilli/chili powder, to taste
12–15 fresh or dried curry leaves, to taste
2 tomatoes, roughly chopped
1 aubergine/eggplant, cut into 2-cm/¾-in. cubes
400-ml/14-oz. can coconut milk
225 g/8 oz. white cabbage, cut into 4-cm/1½-in. pieces
1 teaspoon salt, or to taste
acar awak (see page 161), to serve

SPICE MIX
4 large dried red chillies/chiles
seeds of 4 cardamom pods
4 tablespoons coriander seeds
2 tablespoons cumin seeds
1 tablespoon fennel seeds
10 cloves
20 whole black peppercorns

SERVES 4

For the spice mix, toast the dry spices in a dry frying pan/skillet, taking care not to burn them. Blitz to a powder in a spice grinder. Set aside.

Heat ½ tablespoon of the oil in a large pan or wok, and add the tofu/beancurd pieces. Lightly fry for 4–5 minutes until a little crispy and starting to brown. Place the tofu/beancurd onto paper towels and set aside. Return the pan to high heat with another ½ tablespoon of the oil. Add the okra to the hot pan. Cook for a few minutes until starting to brown, taking care not to overcook. Place the seared okra onto the tofu/beancurd plate and set aside.

Add the onion to the pan along with the remaining ½ tablespoon oil. Fry for about 5 minutes until translucent, then add the garlic, ginger, turmeric and 2 generous tablespoons of the spice mix powder. Sauté over low–medium heat for 3–4 minutes, then add the lemongrass, star anise, cinnamon, chilli/chili powder and curry leaves, mixing well.

Add the tomatoes and aubergine/eggplant, then cook gently for 5 minutes until the tomatoes are breaking down. Add half of the coconut milk and 375 ml/1½ cups water. Bring to a simmer, then add the cabbage and continue to simmer for 7–8 minutes. Finally, add the remaining coconut milk, the tofu/beancurd and okra. Bring the curry back to a gentle simmer for a few minutes and then remove from the heat. Season with salt to taste.

Serve with steamed cauliflower rice or basmati rice, and some acar awak hot pickle on the side.

ACAR AWAK
Seasonal vegetable pickle

This pickle reminds me of Sri Lankan vegetable pickle, and has likely links to this spice trading route between the subcontinent and South-East Asia. This classic Malaysian pickle is tangy, spicy and crunchy. It's definitely not the simplest and quickest pickle to prepare, but well worth the effort as you can vary the vegetables seasonally and it keeps well in the fridge for several weeks. Recipe pictured on page 162.

For the blended spice paste, drain the dried chillies/chiles, keeping back some of the water to add to the paste, if needed. Place all the spice paste ingredients into a blender or food processor and blitz until smooth. Blend in a little of the soaking water if needed. Set aside.

Place the carrot and cucumber pieces into a bowl and add 2 teaspoons of the salt. Mix well and set aside in the fridge for 30 minutes.

Place a pan of water over high heat. Add 50 ml/3½ tablespoons of the vinegar, then add the cauliflower pieces and blanch for 3 minutes. Remove with a slotted spoon and place on paper towels to drain. Now add the green/French beans and cabbage to the boiling water and blanch for 1 minute. Remove with a slotted spoon and place on paper towels to drain.

Remove the carrot and cucumber from the fridge, quickly rinse away the salt and leave to dry on paper towels.

Add the oil to a large pan and place over medium heat. Add the spice paste and cook for 7–8 minutes until the paste starts to darken. Now add the tamarind, soy sauce and vegan fish sauce. Mix well and bring to a simmer. Lower the heat and add the remaining 120 ml/½ cup vinegar, the remaining 1 teaspoon of salt and the date syrup. Check the seasoning and add more salt or syrup if needed. It should be sour, salty and slightly sweet. Remove from the heat and add the peanuts, and then add all the vegetables and the pineapple, if using. Mix everything together really well, and set aside to cool.

Place the pickle into a large sterilized jar and seal. The pickle is ready to eat, but is best left overnight. To serve, place the pickle into a small bowl and sprinkle with toasted sesame seeds.

1 large or 2 medium carrot(s), peeled and cut into 2.5-cm/1-in. batons
1 large cucumber, halved lengthways, deseeded and cut into 2.5-cm/1-in. batons
3 teaspoons salt
170 ml/⅔ cup rice vinegar
¼ medium cauliflower (about 270 g/ 9½ oz.), cut into 2.5-cm/1-in. florets
120 g/4 oz. green/French beans, trimmed and halved
225 g/8 oz. white cabbage, cut into 2.5-cm/1-in. pieces
1 teaspoon culinary/unflavoured coconut oil, or use good-quality vegetable oil (see page 13)
1 teaspoon tamarind pulp
1 tablespoon soy sauce
½ tablespoon vegan fish sauce (see page 13, optional)
80 ml/⅓ cup date syrup, or use pure maple syrup or unrefined coconut sugar
2 tablespoons skinned peanuts, lightly toasted and roughly chopped
3 pineapple rings, cut into small wedges (optional)
1 tablespoon sesame seeds, lightly toasted, to serve

BLENDED SPICE PASTE
4 dried red chillies/chiles, soaked in boiling water for 30 minutes
4 red chillies/chiles, or use extra dried
1 small red onion, quartered
5-cm/2-in. thumb of fresh ginger, peeled, or use 2 heaped tablespoons ginger paste
5-cm/2-in. thumb of fresh galangal, peeled
1 fat garlic clove, or use 1 teaspoon garlic paste
1 lemongrass stick
30 g/1 oz. candle nuts, or use macadamia nuts or cashew nuts
5-cm/2-in. thumb of fresh turmeric, peeled

MAKES 1.4 LITRES/6 CUPS

PERANAKAN TURMERIC & LEMONGRASS NOODLES
with silken tofu

This simplified recipe is based on a Nyonya-style rempah/ spice paste with lemongrass and turmeric. The chewy riceberry or red rice noodles with the silky tofu/beancurd are both creamy and comforting. Riceberry noodles make a highly nutritious alternative to brown rice noodles and are packed with B vitamins and polyphenols, which support heart and circulatory health, and reduce inflammation. This dish can be on the table in under 30 minutes and the paste can be made in advance and kept in the fridge for several weeks. You can also use firm tofu/beancurd or mock chicken, if you prefer.

For the spice paste, drain the dried chillies/chiles, keeping back some of the soaking water to add to the paste while blending, if needed. Blitz all the spice paste ingredients in a blender or food processor, adding a little of the chilli/chile soaking water, if needed, to make a smooth paste.

Add the oil to a pan over medium heat. Add the spice paste and cook gently for 7–8 minutes until fragrant. Add 250 ml/ 1 cup water and half the coconut milk, and bring to a simmer over medium heat. Add the miso, salt and sugar, mix well, then add the spinach leaves. Turn the heat to low, add the remaining coconut milk and carefully add the silken tofu/beancurd pieces. Bring to a gentle simmer for another minute, then remove from the heat.

Soak the noodles in boiling water for 5–10 minutes until soft, then drain in a colander. Divide the noodles between deep bowls, then, taking care not to break the tofu/beancurd pieces, ladle the curry broth over the top. Top with a few spring onions/scallions, chilli/chili oil or chillies/chiles and a wedge of lime.

½ tablespoon culinary/unflavoured coconut oil, or use good-quality vegetable oil
200 ml/scant 1 cup coconut milk
1 heaped teaspoon brown or red miso paste, or use Korean fermented soybean paste/doenjang, or use good-quality vegetable stock powder/bouillon
½–1 teaspoon salt, to taste
1 teaspoon coconut sugar, or use date syrup or pure maple syrup
200 g/4 cups fresh spinach, roughly torn, or use rainbow chard
180 g/6½ oz. silken tofu/beancurd, cut into pieces
160 g/5¾ oz. riceberry or red rice noodles, or use whatever noodles you prefer

REMPAH/SPICE PASTE
8–10 dried red chillies/chiles, soaked in boiling water
1 small brown onion, halved
5-cm/2-in. thumb of fresh turmeric, peeled, or use 1 heaped teaspoon ground turmeric
5-cm/2-in. piece of fresh galangal, peeled and finely chopped, or use fresh ginger
1 tablespoon ground coriander, lightly toasted
4 lemongrass sticks, trimmed and outer layer removed
8–10 candle nuts, or use macadamia or cashew nuts, soaked for 1 hour and drained
½ teaspoon salt
½ teaspoon white pepper

TO SERVE
2 spring onions/scallions, sliced at an angle
chilli/chili oil, or use 2 fresh chillies/ chiles, thinly sliced
lime wedges

SERVES 2

KARIPAP PUSING
Curry puffs

350 g/2⅔ cups plain/all-purpose flour, or use gluten-free flour, plus extra for dusting
¼ teaspoon ground turmeric
75 g/2¾ oz. block-style vegan baking margarine, cut up and chilled
1 tablespoon vegan egg replacement, such as Orgran, mixed with 3 tablespoons water
1 teaspoon salt
1 tablespoon good-quality vegetable oil (see page 13), plus extra for brushing
100 ml/generous ⅓ cup cold water

FILLING
1 tablespoon black peppercorns
2 teaspoons fennel seeds
1 star anise
5-cm/2-in. cinnamon stick
2 tablespoons culinary/unflavoured coconut oil, or use good-quality vegetable oil (see page 13)
2 banana shallots, finely chopped
2.5-cm/1-in. thumb of fresh ginger, peeled and finely chopped, or use 1 heaped tablespoon ginger paste
250 g/9 oz. white potatoes, peeled and cut into 1-cm/½-in. cubes
1 large sweet potato, peeled and cut into 1-cm/½-in. cubes (about 250 g/ 2 cups)
1 teaspoon salt
2 brown onions, finely chopped
large handful of freshly chopped coriander/cilantro
1 large spring onion/scallion, thinly sliced

baking sheet, lined with parchment

MAKES 20

Malaysian curry puffs are an incredibly popular snack, usually stuffed with spiced potato, either with or without chicken. They remind me a little of samosas, with a similarity in toasted spices, and especially when they're fried. I try not to eat fried food very often, as it can be a highly inflammatory food to the body, especially when eaten in excess. These flaky, baked little puffs are lighter, but equally delicious.

Start by making the filling. Place the dry spices into a small frying pan/skillet and lightly toast until fragrant. Place in a spice grinder and blend to a fine powder. Add 2 tablespoons of water to the mixture and blend again to make a paste. Set aside.

In a wok or large, deep frying pan/skillet, add the oil, shallots and ginger. Place over low–medium heat and cook gently until the shallots are just translucent. Add the spice mixture, and continue to cook for another minute. Now add the white potatoes plus 300 ml/1¼ cups water. Mix well and bring to a simmer. Reduce the heat to medium and cook for 5 minutes, then add the sweet potato and continue to cook for another 10–12 minutes until the potatoes are soft and the mixture is almost dry. Add the remaining filling ingredients and mix well. Set aside to cool.

Preheat the oven to 180°C (350°F) Gas 4.

Place 100 g/¾ cup of the flour into a bowl along with the turmeric. Rub in the margarine to make a rough breadcrumb-like texture. Knead until a dough forms, then cover and set aside.

Place the remaining flour into a bowl with the vegan egg mixture, salt, oil and cold water. Combine to form another firm dough.

Divide each dough mixture into five large balls. Take one of the white dough balls and flatten in the palm of your had. Place one of the yellow dough balls in the middle and wrap the outer dough around the outside to make a large dough ball. Repeat with the remaining dough balls, so you have five large dough balls.

Sprinkle a work surface with flour and, using a rolling pin, flatten each ball to a large oval shape, then roll to make a long strip. Cut each piece of dough into four pieces, and roll each piece again until you have four roughly oval shapes, 5 mm/¼ in. thick.

Place a spoonful of filling into the centre of a pastry piece and fold to make a half-moon shape, pinching and folding around the edge. Repeat with the remaining pastry and filling, arrange on the lined baking sheet and brush with oil. Bake in the preheated oven for 20–25 minutes until golden brown. Serve warm.

HAKKA-STYLE BRAISED & STUFFED TOFU/ BEANCURD

400-g/14-oz. block firm tofu/beancurd
1 teaspoon culinary/unflavoured
  coconut oil, or use good-quality
  vegetable oil (see page 13)

FILLING
8 large pieces of dried porcini
  mushrooms, soaked in boiling water
  for 1 hour, or use shiitake or any
  dried mushrooms (if using whole,
  use 2 mushrooms)
2 tablespoons vegan mince
1 teaspoon soy sauce
2 teaspoons Shaoxing wine
1 spring onion/scallion, thinly sliced
¼ teaspoon brown sugar

BRAISING STOCK
1 tablespoon vegan oyster sauce,
  aka mushroom stir-fry sauce
1 tablespoon soy sauce
¼ teaspoon white pepper

SAUCE
1 teaspoon culinary/unflavoured
  coconut oil, or use good-quality
  vegetable oil (see page 13)
1 fat garlic clove, finely chopped,
  or use 1 teaspoon garlic paste
1 small chilli/chile, finely chopped,
  or use large pinch of dried chilli
  flakes/hot red pepper flakes
1 teaspoon tomato purée/paste
1 tablespoon soy sauce
1 spring onion/scallion, thinly sliced and
  separated into white and green parts
1 teaspoon cornflour/cornstarch,
  or use tapioca/potato starch

SERVES 4 AS SMALL PLATES

As vegetarians, we ate a lot of Chinese food in Malaysia. We love roti canai and the trays upon trays of veggies piled up in the food halls, but it can get a bit monotonous when you don't eat meat or fish. So we always seek out great Indian Malaysian food (there's a huge southern influence like dosas and roti across Malaysia and Singapore), and also rather magnificent Chinese food. Probably some of the best vegan Chinese food we've ever enjoyed. Much of Malaysian Chinese food has roots in Nyonya cooking (Chinese-Malay and Singaporean), but there are also many other Chinese food influences in this region, like Hakka cuisine originating from Hong Kong, but which can be found across Taiwan, Indonesia, Thailand, Malaysia and Singapore.

For the filling, drain the soaked mushrooms, preserving the soaking liquid for later. Finely chop the mushrooms, and add to a small bowl along with all the other filling ingredients. Mix well.

Cut the firm tofu/beancurd into large cubes, at least 3 cm/1¼ in. wide, keeping the full depth of the tofu/beancurd slab. Using a paring knife, carefully carve out a hole in the centre of each cube, making a tofu/beancurd pocket to fill with stuffing mix. Try not to cut through the bottom, you want to create a small, empty box shape with thick sides.

Stuff the filling into the tofu/beancurd pieces, gently pressing down so it's tightly filled.

Next, strain the leftover mushroom soaking liquid through a fine sieve/strainer and combine it with the braising stock ingredients.

Add the oil to a lidded frying pan/skillet, and place the stuffed tofu/beancurd into the pan, stuffing-side down. It should stay in place if firmly stuffed, and brown gently for 1–2 minutes, then carefully turn and fry on the other side until nicely browned. Add three-quarters of the mushroom braising stock mixture and bring to a simmer. Half-cover with the lid and cook until the broth has been absorbed and fully evaporated.

Meanwhile, make the sauce. Heat the oil in a pan and add the garlic. Fry for 1–2 minutes, then add the chilli/chile, tomato purée/paste, soy sauce, spring onion/scallion whites, 125 ml/ ½ cup water and remaining mushroom stock. Make a paste with the cornflour/cornstarch and a little water, then add to the sauce to thicken. Simmer for 2 minutes until fragrant and the cornflour/cornstarch is cooked through.

Serve the stuffed tofu/beancurd with sauce poured all over and top with a final sprinkle of the spring onion/scallion greens.

KUIH SAGO
Malaysian sago cake with rose

This naturally gluten-free Nyonya treat is softly chewy and melts in the mouth. It's not too sweet with a gentle hint of rose. A kind of coconutty Turkish delight without the gelatine. These tapioca/sago based cakes make a delightful after-dinner treat, but are eaten at all times of the day. I find them rather palate-cleansing.

Pandan is popular in both savoury and sweet food in Malaysian and Indonesian cooking (pandan ice cream is a firm favourite everywhere). This recipe uses the leaf to steep the flavour, before it is removed. This is the easiest way to use pandan.

You can also make these cakes as purely pandan, by substituting the rose water for pandan juice. These sweets will be bright green instead of pink. You can make your own pandan juice, as shop-bought extract is usually a very poor substitute, where the difference is night and day. Recipe pictured on page 163.

40 g/½ cup coarse desiccated/dried unsweetened shredded coconut
2 tablespoons rose essence
1 tablespoon beetroot/beet juice, to taste (drained from a pack of cooked beetroot)
3 generous tablespoons pure maple syrup or unrefined coconut sugar (you can also use date syrup but it will colour the cakes a little darker)
pinch of salt
2 pandan leaves, tied into knots
85 g/½ cup tapioca pearls/sago

15 x 10-cm/6 x 4-in. baking pan or heatproof dish, greased and lined with parchment

MAKES 18 PIECES

Place the coconut in a small bowl and cover with boiling water. Leave to soak for 15 minutes until softened, then drain in a fine sieve/strainer and set aside.

Add 500 ml/2 cups of cold water to a small pan with the rose essence, beetroot/beet juice, maple syrup, salt and the knotted pandan leaves. Add the tapioca pearls and mix to ensure that the pearls are not stuck together.

Place the pan over medium–high heat and bring to the boil. Reduce the heat to low and simmer gently, stirring occasionally to prevent the mixture sticking to the bottom of the pan. Cook for 20 minutes until the mixture is very thick and sticky. The pearls will still have a small white dot in the centre. Remove from the heat and carefully remove and discard the pandan knots.

Pour the mixture into the prepared baking pan or dish and smooth the top. Cover the top of the mixture with a square of parchment.

Place the pan or dish in a large steamer over a pan of boiling water. If using a metal basket-type steamer in a pan, ensure the pan lid leaves a small gap, to allow some of the steam to escape. Steam the cake for 20–25 minutes.

Remove the cake and blot away any excess water with paper towels. Leave to cool, then place in the fridge for at least 1 hour. Using the parchment, lift the cake out of the dish. With a sharp knife, slice the cake into about 18 small pieces.

Place the coconut on a plate and, taking one piece at a time, gently coat the cake pieces in the coconut. Store in the fridge in an airtight container, for up to 1 week. Allow to come to room temperature before serving on a banana leaf.

Left: Tea plantations as far as the eye can see, Cameron Highlands, Peninsular Malaysia.

TOASTED COCONUT, & MANGO ICE CREAM

This is a very simple recipe for a delicious plant-based ice cream. It has a toasty depth of creamy flavour, complemented by the tangy mango chunks.

400-ml/14-oz. can coconut milk (minimum 80% coconut)
40 g/¼ cup coconut sugar
½ vanilla pod/bean, seeds removed, or use 1 teaspoon vanilla paste or 2 teaspoons pure vanilla extract
3 tablespoons desiccated/dried unsweetened shredded coconut, lightly toasted, plus extra to serve (optional)
425-g/15-oz. can mango slices, in juice (not syrup), cut into 1.5-cm/½-in. cubes

SERVES 6

To make the ice cream, place the coconut milk in a small pan and add the sugar and vanilla. If using a pod/bean, add the scraped pod/bean, too. Place over low heat and gently warm until all the sugar dissolves. Remove from the heat and discard the vanilla pod/bean. Add the toasted coconut and mix well.

Pour the mixture into a wide tub with a lid and place in the freezer for 40 minutes. Remove and, using a fork, mix well ensuring you scrape any icy bits from the edges. Add the mango pieces and mix well. Return the ice cream to the freezer for another 30 minutes, then repeat the mixing process and freeze again until ready to serve.

Remove from the freezer 20 minutes before serving. Top with some extra toasted coconut flakes, if you like.

Left: Prepped bags of fresh, tropical fruit at a street-food stall, Penang, Malaysia.

Indonesia

Nasi campur was the first actual street food dish we ate in Indonesia. After being unceremoniously dumped off our local public bus, we found ourselves in the middle of nowhere, with two Argentinians and a highly anxious New Yorker. After begging the driver not to leave us, he agreed to call his friend with a 'bemo' taxi to take us to Samosir lake. It was now going dark and Nick the New Yorker was getting more strung out by the second. True to the driver's word, a battered old Honda van pulled up and bounced us along for several hours to reach the boat for the island. We arrived shortly before midnight, and none of us had eaten anything other than a few of Nick's saltine crackers.

I wandered up to a small wooden house, close to the jetty, with a plastic chair and a few stools around a table. Behind the simple table counter, a small glass cabinet held four large bowls on two shelves, with a reassuring little fly curtain behind. The greens looked a little sludgy but my hunger was driving my confidence. With my Bahasa phrase book in hand, I asked if any of the bowls were vegetarian, and she nodded, so we ordered a plate of food to share – greens, rice and sambal. Gaby and Diego decided they would give it a try too. Nick shuffled off with his saltine crackers to sit by the jetty, whilst we sat around on stools enjoying our impromptu supper.

Lee and I were lucky enough to stumble into Sumatra during the early 90s, long before the island was devastated by the 2003 earthquake and tsunami. We had never visited Asia before, and yet somehow made the bold decision that we should head straight for Shangri-La. We heard about this very remote guesthouse from a close friend. These Toba Batak-style huts, with their boat like architecture and upsweeping roof ridges sit along the banks of a volcanic island in Lake Toba, North Sumatra. It took us six days, with one overnight train, two ferries and two quite scary bus journeys, followed by a six-hour hike to Amborita before we found Palmi's place. And it was worth every terrifying second of the journey!

We've since returned to Indonesia numerous times during the following decades, and every time we visit new places and experience yet more incredible Indonesian hospitality. With over 900 inhabited islands (the total is estimated at 17508), this archipelago is scattered with an incredible diversity of cultures and ethnicities (and food). I am continually fascinated by the way that Islam (and Christianity) have integrated with ancient island cultures and practices, whilst long-standing Hindu and Buddhist influences remain strong, including on Bali, Java and Lombok, as well as Kalimantan, Sulawesi and north Sumatra.

There is so much beauty in Indonesia, it would take many lifetimes to truly explore, and I hope to spend some of what's left of mine in Kalimantan, Sulawesi and, if I'm truly lucky, Raja Ampat.

If I had no ties and could live anywhere in the world, I would live in Lombok. It has always held my heart, with its laid back beaches, vibrant underwater life, friendly villages and towns, and an epic volcanic landscape dominated by mount Rinjani, the second highest in Indonesia.

Clockwise from top left: Volcanic landscape, Bandung, Java; Threading marigolds, Ubud, Bali; Ganesha shrine, Ubud, Bali; Traditional Hindu-Balinese morning offering to the gods; Batak-style house, Samosir Island, Lake Toba.

BALI BREAKFAST STACK *Baked corn & kale fritters with spicy ratatouille, crispy tempeh & tamarind sauce*

Ubud is the home of the holy and the wholesome. The quiet main street of our previous visit was transformed into a maze of crowded roads, packed with noisy gridlocked traffic and lined with high-end hotels, restaurants and boutiques. The town has grown so much in size, that I had trouble even remembering where we had been before. Nothing looked familiar. But as soon as we exited these busy main streets, the old Ubud was alive and well behind the modern facades. Fields of rice paddies surrounding traditional walled houses and villages connected by narrow walkways and lanes, spilling over with hibiscus, bougainvillaea and frangipani. Many outer areas of Ubud are thriving with vibrant and creative communities, including active environmental policies (such as recycling projects and field-to-table farming). Ubud is also home to some of the best yoga centres in the world.

We had a plan to sign up for another week of intensive yoga practice, and visit the incredible Green Village for some retreat research. By some beautiful accident, our humble but extraordinarily beautiful AirBnB was just a short hop from one of these studios. As we wandered through the lanes and waterways to our morning class, we passed the Yellow Flower Café. A remarkable little place nestled on the hilltop overlooking the lush Campuhan valley below, serving kombucha, traditional Indonesian food and pan-Pacific-inspired brunches with local produce. Needless to say, this café became our regular post-class haunt.

This recipe can be served for brunch or as a light meal at any time of day. The fritters can be cooked then chilled or frozen, then reheated in a medium–hot oven. The spicy ratatouille also freezes well, so it is worthwhile doubling the batch. The tamarind sauce will keep for several weeks in the fridge, stored in a sterilized airtight jar.

300 g/generous 2 cups canned or fresh corn (or substitute sprouted mung beans or beansprouts)
4–5 kale leaves, stems removed and thinly sliced, or use other dark cabbage
1 small red onion, thinly sliced
1 spring onion/scallion, thinly sliced
75 g/scant ⅔ cup rice flour
75 g/scant ⅔ cup gram flour (chickpea/garbanzo bean flour), sifted
200 ml/scant 1 cup cold water
1 teaspoon ground cumin
1 teaspoon freshly grated turmeric root, or use ½ teaspoon ground turmeric
1 teaspoon salt
small handful of freshly chopped coriander/cilantro

RATATOUILLE
1 tablespoon olive oil
2 fat garlic cloves, finely chopped, or use 2 teaspoons garlic paste
½ teaspoon dried chilli flakes/hot red pepper flakes, or use chilli/chili powder
1 teaspoon salt
1 large aubergine/eggplant, cut into 1.5-cm/½-in. cubes
½ red (bell) pepper, cut into 1.5-cm/½-in. pieces
½ green (bell) pepper, cut into 1.5-cm/½-in. pieces
1 small courgette/zucchini, cut into 1.5-cm/½-in. cubes
4 large tomatoes, cored and roughly chopped, or use a 400-g/14-oz. can plum tomatoes

TEMPEH BACON
80 g/3 oz. tempeh, thinly sliced into 8 pieces
2 tablespoons soy sauce, or use tamari
1 teaspoon culinary/unflavoured coconut oil, or use good-quality vegetable oil (see page 13)

TAMARIND SAUCE
2 tablespoons tamarind pulp plus 2 tablespoons water, or use 1 teaspoon tamarind concentrate plus 4 tablespoons water
2 tablespoons coconut sugar, or use unrefined brown sugar

TO SERVE
2 large handfuls rocket/arugula
    or lamb's lettuce (optional)
handful of coriander/cilantro
sambal balado (see page 197)

*baking sheet, lined with parchment
and lightly greased*

SERVES 4

Start by preparing the ratatouille. Add the oil to a heavy-bottomed pan, then add the garlic and place over low heat. Gently cook the garlic for 2 minutes, then add the dried chilli flakes/hot red pepper flakes and salt. Add all the vegetables except the tomatoes, and mix well. Turn up the heat to medium and sauté all the vegetables until starting to soften and brown on the edges. Now add the tomatoes and a splash of cold water (or tomato juice if using canned). Bring to a simmer and cook over low heat for 20–30 minutes.

To make the fritters, add all the ingredients to a large bowl and, using one clean hand, mix well until everything is combined. The mixture should be a thick porridge-like consistency.

Preheat the oven to 190°C (375°F) Gas 5.

Place heaped tablespoons of the mixture at even spaces on the lined and greased baking sheet. Wet the spoon and gently flatten the mixture to make little patties. Bake in the oven for 20–25 minutes, turning once after 10–15 minutes of cooking.

For the tempeh bacon, place the tempeh slices on a plate and cover in the soy sauce. Set aside for 5–10 minutes to marinate. Place a large frying pan/skillet over high heat and add the oil. Gently lay the slices into the pan and fry until crispy brown, about 2–3 minutes on each side. Drain on paper towels and set aside (or place on baking sheet in the oven to keep warm).

To make the tamarind sauce, add the ingredients to a small pan and bring to simmer. Cook until the liquid has reduced by half, and you have a thickened dark sauce. Set aside to cool.

To serve, place a small handful of rocket or lamb's lettuce (if using) in the centre of each plate. Next, stack three or four fritters on top of the greens, then add 2–3 tablespoons of ratatouille on top. Drizzle over the tamarind sauce, making a circle around the stack. Top the stack with a couple of slices of crispy tempeh and a few coriander/cilantro leaves. Serve immediately with a side of sambal.

Above: Dragon bridge, Mandala Suci Wenara Wana/Monkey Forest Sanctuary, Ubud, Bali.

SIMPLE NASI CAMPUR
Tempeh brittle, purple potato curry & coconut kale stir-fry

Indonesia's answer to India's thali. This selection plate means 'mixed rice', simply a plate of rice with three or four different dishes. It's a generic term used across Indonesia and Malaysia. Nasi padang is a type of nasi campur, originating from the city of Padang in West Sumatra, where the mixed rice plate was served as a huge banquet alongside multiple curries made with meat, fish and vegetables, plus spicy sambals, peanuts and eggs. The Dutch colonialists adored this Minangkabau banqueting, which they called 'rijstaffel' or 'rice-table'. Rijstaffel restaurants are incredibly popular throughout the Netherlands, and a closer foodie experience for most Europeans. Go hungry and be prepared for 15–20 dishes to be laid around the table.

This recipe is a simplified little taste of nasi campur to make at home. The moreish tempeh brittle recipe uses a significant amount of (unrefined) sugars, so the portion should be a very small part of the whole platter, or give this a miss if you are trying to reduce your sugar intake and simply fry some soy-marinated tempeh instead (see page 176). The kale stir-fry and simple curry are super-quick to prepare. You could also add other Indonesian elements like loaded cassava fries (see page 188), manadu 'woku' curry (see page 193) or Indonesian corn 'ribs' (see page 190), if you want to create a larger rijstaffel.

TEMPEH BRITTLE

250 g/9 oz. tempeh
**1 tablespoon plus 1 teaspoon culinary/
   unflavoured coconut oil, or use
   good-quality vegetable oil
   (see page 13)**
**1-cm/½-in. thumb of fresh ginger,
   peeled and finely chopped
   (about 2 teaspoons), or use
   1 teaspoon ginger paste**
2 tablespoons coconut sugar
**1 tablespoon date syrup, or use
   pure maple syrup or unrefined
   coconut sugar**
3 tablespoons soy sauce
large pinch of salt

baking sheet, lined with parchment

MAKES 6 SMALL PORTIONS

Preheat the oven to 190°C (375°F) Gas 5.

Cut the tempeh into 6 mm/¼ in. thick slices, then slice into 1 cm/½ in. wide small pieces (the length will be the width of your tempeh block).

Place a wide frying pan/skillet over high heat with 1 tablespoon of the oil. When the oil is very hot, add the tempeh pieces. Fry for 8–10 minutes until crispy and brown on all sides. Remove and place on paper towels to drain.

In the same pan, add another teaspoon of oil and add the ginger. Turn down heat to low and cook gently for 2 minutes, then add the remaining ingredients (except the tempeh). Bring the mixture to a low simmer until a thick syrup starts to form, then add the tempeh pieces. Mix well to coat all the pieces and fry gently until the liquid is reduced and sticky.

Lay the pieces onto the lined baking sheet and bake in the preheated oven for 10 minutes until crispy and nicely browned. Remove and set aside to cool. The pieces will then become more brittle and crunchy.

COCONUT KALE STIR-FRY

1 tablespoon extra-virgin coconut
    oil, or use culinary/unflavoured
    coconut oil or good-quality
    vegetable oil (see page 13)
7–8 curry leaves
1 large brown onion, thinly sliced
3 fat garlic cloves, thinly sliced
½ teaspoon ground turmeric
7.5–10-cm/3–4-in. cinnamon stick
250–300-g/9–10½-oz. bunch or
    200g-g/7-oz. bag of kale, thick
    stems removed and thinly sliced
75 g/1 cup desiccated/dried
    unsweetened shredded coconut,
    soaked in boiling water for
    15 minutes
2 green chillies/chiles, chopped
½–1 teaspoon salt, to taste
freshly squeezed juice of 1 lime
    (about ½ tablespoon)

SERVES 6

Place a wok or large frying pan/
skillet over high heat. Add the oil
and then add the curry leaves, frying
for 20–30 seconds. Now add the
onion, garlic, turmeric and cinnamon.
Turn down the heat to medium–low,
and gently stir-fry for 3–4 minutes
until the onions are softened and
the garlic is golden brown.

Add the kale and turn up the
heat to medium–high. Stir-fry for
8–10 minutes until the kale starts
to soften, depending on how
crunchy you prefer your kale. Drain
the desiccated/dried unsweetened
shredded coconut and squeeze out
any excess water. Add the coconut
and chillies/chiles to the pan, mix
well and cook for 1 minute more.

Season with salt and remove from
the heat. Add the lime juice and mix
well. Serve immediately.

PURPLE POTATO CURRY

½ tablespoon culinary/unflavoured
    coconut oil, or use good-quality
    vegetable oil (see page 13)
1 large brown onion, finely chopped
2 fat garlic cloves, finely chopped,
    or use 2 teaspoons garlic paste
4–8 small red chillies/chiles, to taste
¼ teaspoon chilli/chili powder
1 teaspoon ground cumin
1 tablespoon ground coriander
400-g/14-oz. can plum tomatoes
250 g/9 oz. purple potatoes, peeled
    and cubed, or use new potatoes
250 g/9 oz. firm tofu/beancurd,
    cubed (and lightly baked if you
    prefer)
½–1 teaspoon salt, to taste

SERVES 6

Place a large frying pan/skillet or
wok over medium–high heat and
add the oil. Add the onion and sauté
for 4–5 minutes until translucent.
Add the garlic, cook for 1 minute,
then add the chillies/chiles and
ground spices. Add the tomatoes
(and juices) plus 3½ tablespoons
water, then squash the tomatoes
to a pulp. Simmer for a few minutes,
then remove from the heat.

Using a stick blender, blitz until
smooth. Return the pan to high
heat and add the potatoes. Place
a lid on the pan, turn the heat
down to low and simmer the
potatoes for 20–25 minutes
until soft but not falling apart.

Add the tofu/beancurd pieces.
Season with salt and add a little
more water if needed. This curry
can be reheated when needed.

TO SERVE

cooked black rice
3–4 tablespoons sambal balado
    (see page 197)
3–4 tablespoons red-skinned
    peanuts, lightly toasted,
    or use cashew nuts
freshly chopped coriander/cilantro
rice crackers (see page 136)

To serve the nasi campur
individually, place some cooked
black rice in the centre of a plate
(or on a banana leaf if you like).
Add a large spoonful of each of the
dishes around the outside, plus a
spoonful of sambal balado (or hot
chilli/chili sambal) and a spoonful
of toasted red skinned peanuts.
Sprinkle the potato curry with a
little fresh coriander/cilantro and
add a few rice crackers, if you like.
Indonesian rice crackers are fried,
so I prefer to serve with baked
Vietnamese-style crackers for
a healthier option.

WATERMELON SALAD

500 g/1 lb. 2 oz. prepared watermelon, seeds removed and cut into 2-cm/¾-in. cubes
½ Granny Smith apple, cored and sliced into thin sticks
1 tablespoon crispy shallots (see page 82, but use shallots instead of onions and garlic)
handful of Indonesian lemon basil, or use Italian basil with 1 teaspoon lemon juice
12–15 mint leaves, roughly torn
½ teaspoon white sesame seeds, lightly toasted

SAUCE
70 g/½ cup raspberries
60 ml/¼ cup balsamic vinegar
1 tablespoon coconut sugar
1 tablespoon raw cacao powder, or use ¾ tablespoon unsweetened cocoa powder
1 teaspoon chilli/chili sauce, or use sambol olek

SERVES 4–5 AS A STARTER

This recipe was inspired by one of the best vegan meals of my life. I heard about Hujan Locale because the chef proprietor happens to do consultancy work for the same UK restaurant group that I've worked with since graduating from MasterChef. I had heard many great things about Will's numerous restaurants in Bali, and we were lucky enough to visit three of them. But it was Hujan that stole my foodie heart, with its inspirational farm-to-table menu harnessing local and ancient Balinese produce, with a vegan menu that makes your heart flutter. The fact that the restaurant is a designer's dream just added to this incredible experience.

I love watermelon salads but this one is very special indeed. Bali produces some incredible cocoa (and coffee) and my fellow diners were equally enthralled by the combination of cocoa in the moreish, lightly spiced, sweet and savoury dressing. My version uses raspberries as a sweet-sour note in the dressing.

To make the sauce, place the raspberries, balsamic and coconut sugar in a small pan. Place over medium heat and bring to a low simmer. Cook gently until slightly reduced and the fruit has completely broken down. Remove from the heat and pour through a fine sieve/strainer into a small bowl. Use the back of a spoon to push through all the sauce and pulp, and discard all the seeds. Add the remaining sauce ingredients to the bowl and whisk until well combined. Set aside.

Add the prepared watermelon, apple and crispy shallots to a large mixing bowl. Add most of the Indonesian lemon basil and mint leaves, keeping back a few to garnish. Add the sauce and, using your hands or kitchen gloves, mix well so all the ingredients are well combined and all the fruit is coated in the sticky sauce.

To serve, lay the salad onto a large platter, and scatter with the toasted sesame seeds and remaining herbs. Serve immediately.

JAVANESE PEPES TAHU
Spiced tofu/beancurd in banana leaves

This traditional Indonesian dish hails from West Java, and consists of spicy tofu/beancurd wrapped in a banana leaf and then steamed or grilled/broiled. This filling is easy to prep ahead and keeps in the fridge for a few days. The cooked parcels also make great picnic or travel food, with a little bag of sticky rice and sambal.

280 g/10 oz. tofu/beancurd
1 red (bell) pepper, cut into 2-cm/¾-in. pieces
2 spring onions/scallions, sliced
handful of Indonesian lemon basil, or use Thai basil, or use any basil that you have, roughly torn
1 large tomato, roughly chopped
4 pieces of banana leaf, cut into 25-cm/10-in. squares, or substitute greaseproof paper, wrapping the parcel twice over

REMPAH/SPICE PASTE
1 small red onion, quartered
2–3 fat garlic cloves, to taste, or use 2–3 teaspoons garlic paste
1 tablespoon date syrup, or use pure maple syrup or unrefined coconut sugar
2–3 large red chillies/chiles
1 teaspoon salt
4-cm/1½-in. thumb of fresh turmeric, peeled, or use 1 teaspoon ground turmeric
4 macadamia nuts, or use 6–7 cashew nuts

TO SERVE
raw vegetable crudités
sambal balado (see page 197)

MAKES 4

Preheat the oven to 200°C (400°F) Gas 6.

Add all the rempah/spice paste ingredients to a blender or food processor and blitz until smooth.

Crumble the tofu/beancurd into a large bowl, then add the (bell) pepper, spring onions/scallions, basil, tomato and the spice paste. Using your hands, mix everything together so it is well combined.

Lay the banana leaves onto a work surface and clean them with a damp cloth. Add one-quarter of the tofu/beancurd mixture to the bottom quarter of each leaf and then roll over and wrap each one, so the filling is securely encased. Tie some string/twine around to secure the packages, if needed.

Lay the parcels onto a baking sheet, and roast in the preheated oven for 30 minutes. Alternatively, to steam the parcels, place a large steamer over a pan of boiling water and place the parcels inside. Cover and steam for 25–30 minutes. You can also grill/broil the parcels, or cook them on a barbeque/outdoor grill on each side for 10 minutes.

Serve warm with some sticky rice or raw vegetable crudités, with some sambal balado on the side.

MEE BAKSO
Indonesian-style noodle soup with mock meatballs

Bakso are Indonesian meatballs, mostly served in an aromatic noodle soup (mee). Reportedly one of President Obama's favourite dishes. There are no definitive recipes for this dish, which can be made using beef, chicken or seafood, and like Malaysia's famous laksa, it varies significantly across this diverse archipelago.

To make the broth, place a large, deep pan over high heat and add the oil and garlic. Fry the garlic until just starting to brown, then add the ginger, cardamom seeds, star anise and cinnamon stick. Turn the heat down to medium and cook the aromatics for another 2–3 minutes.

Add the onions and celery, and cook over high heat until starting to brown. Add the remaining broth ingredients, mix and bring to the boil. Reduce the heat and simmer for 20–30 minutes. Remove the pan from the heat. Let stand for 30–40 minutes. Strain the broth through a colander to remove the large pieces of vegetables and beans (discard or save to blend up into a soup).

Place the noodles in a large pan of boiling water, simmer for 2 minutes, then drain and set aside in a bowl of cold water. (If using rice noodles, soak them in boiling water for 10 minutes until softened. Rinse and set aside in cold water.)

Add the oil to a large, deep pan or wok and place over medium heat. Add the mock meatballs and fry until lightly browned all over. Now pour in the broth and bring to a simmer. If using less tender leaves, like spring cabbage, add the greens now and cook for 1–2 minutes before adding the beansprouts; if using tender leaves like chard or spinach, remove the pan from the heat and add the leaves and beansprouts (keeping back a small handful for garnish), allowing them to wilt in the hot broth.

When ready to serve, refresh the noodles by pouring boiling water over the top and divide them between four bowls. Carefully divide the greens and meatballs between the bowls, laying the greens in one corner and adding more broth so that the noodles are well covered. Add some crispy onions, the rest of the beansprouts and a spoonful of sambal, then scatter with some fresh coriander/cilantro leaves. Serve immediately with lime slices and extra sambal on the side, if you like.

220 g/8 oz. thick dried yellow noodles, or use rice stick noodles (3–5 mm/⅛–¼in.) for gluten-free

½ tablespoon culinary/unflavoured coconut oil, or use avocado, refined olive oil or pomace oil

18–20 vegan mock 'meatballs', beef-style works best

about 16 rainbow chard or spinach leaves, or other tender greens

large handful of fresh beansprouts, or use ½ jar, drained and rinsed

2 tablespoons crispy onions (see page 82)

3–4 tablespoons sambol olek

small handful of coriander/cilantro

lime slices, to serve (optional)

BROTH

½ tablespoon culinary/unflavoured coconut oil, or good-quality vegetable oil (see page 13)

4 fat garlic cloves, finely chopped, or use 4 teaspoons garlic paste

5-cm/2-in. thumb of fresh ginger, peeled and finely chopped, or use 2 heaped tablespoons ginger paste

seeds of 2–3 green cardamom pods

3 star anise

7.5–10-cm/3–4-in. cinnamon stick

2 brown onions, thickly sliced

2 sticks of celery, leaves included, thickly sliced

½ tablespoon date syrup, or use pure maple syrup or coconut sugar

1 teaspoon freshly ground white pepper

¼ teaspoon yeast extract, or use 1 teaspoon brown miso

6–7 dried porcini mushrooms, or use dried shiitake or any dried wild mushroom

1 tablespoon vegan fish sauce (see page 13), or use Henderson's Relish (optional)

1 tablespoon soy sauce

400-g/14-oz. can cannellini beans, drained and rinsed (optional)

1.5 litres/quarts water

SERVES 4

LOADED CASSAVA FRIES *with gado gado-style peanut sauce*

1 kg/2 lb. 4 oz. cassava (about 2 small or 1 large)

2–3 tablespoons culinary/unflavoured coconut oil, melted, or use good-quality vegetable oil (see page 13)

3 tablespoons vegan mayonnaise

freshly squeezed juice of 1 lime

2–3 tablespoons sriracha, or use another chilli/chili sauce

handful of freshly chopped coriander/cilantro

1 tablespoon crispy shallots (see page 82, but use shallots instead of onions and garlic), or use 1 spring onion/scallion, thinly sliced at an angle

1 large red chilli/chile, thinly sliced at an angle

½ teaspoon black sesame seeds

PEANUT SAUCE

3 tablespoons crunchy peanut butter (if it is sugar-free, add ½ tablespoon date syrup or pure maple syrup), or use almond or cashew butter

1½ teaspoons garam masala

1 teaspoon dried chilli flakes/hot red pepper flakes

1-cm/½-in. thumb of fresh ginger, peeled and finely chopped (about 2 teaspoons), or use 1 teaspoon ginger paste

1 small garlic clove, finely chopped

½–1 teaspoon salt, to taste

baking sheet, lined with parchment and lightly oiled

SERVES 4 AS A SIDE

Gado gado is usually served as a plate of steamed and raw veggies, drizzled with a fragrant and spicy peanut sauce. You can also use the peanut sauce as a simple marinade on roasted veggies, tofu/beancurd or mock chicken, or as a base for a nutty noodle soup.

Loaded fries are a big trend in UK street food, but definitely not a healthy option when deep-fried. This recipe gives them a healthier little Indonesian twist using cassava, which is a hugely popular vegetable across the archipelago. Cassava (or yuca as it tends to be known in the Caribbean and stateside) has a lower glycaemic index than standard potatoes, so won't spike your blood sugar as heavily. This dish is all about the toppings and sprinkles, which you can adjust to whatever you have available.

To make the sauce, place a small pan over medium heat. Add all the sauce ingredients except the salt, plus 200 ml/scant 1 cup of cold water. Mix well and bring to a simmer, cooking gently for about 8 minutes until slightly reduced and thickened. Season with salt to taste, then set aside.

Prepare the cassava. Remove the ends, then cut the root into three or four large round pieces, approx. 5–7.5 cm/2–3 in. long. Using a sharp knife, peel the tough outer layer. If the root is larger and fresh, you can score down one side of the skin of each piece, then peel away the tough outer skin layer.

Place a large pot of boiling water over high heat and add the cassava rounds. Lower the heat and simmer for 15–20 minutes until just tender. Drain in a colander and set the pieces aside to cool on paper towels.

Preheat the oven to 220°C (425°F) Gas 7.

Once cooled, slice the cassava rounds lengthways down the centre to reveal the middle and carefully remove the narrow core. Now slice the pieces into fingers.

Arrange the cassava fries on the lined and oiled baking sheet and drizzle with the oil. Bake in the preheated oven for 15 minutes until golden brown and crispy, turning halfway through.

Mix together the mayonnaise and the lime juice in a small bowl.

When the fries are cooked, place in a wide bowl or on a platter. Drizzle the peanut sauce over the top. Then, using a small squeezy bottle or spoon, drizzle the mayonnaise and the sriracha over the top, making zig-zag patterns. Serrve sprinkled with coriander/cilantro, crispy shallots, chilli/chile and sesame seeds.

SAYUR ASEM
Indonesian sour vegetable stew

This Sundanese dish is a favourite in Java and very easy to prepare. Tangy and savoury with a little heat, you can include whatever vegetables you might have or that are in season. The chunky vegetables are cooked in a spiced tamarind soup base, and make a hearty lunch. Whilst not traditional, I like to add some cooked quinoa alongside the stew or add it to the bottom of the bowl, and ladle the soup on top for a more substantial dinner. You can also serve this with rice crackers and some extra sambal, if you like.

Place all the spice paste ingredients into a blender or food processor and blitz to a smooth paste.

Add the oil to a large wok or pan and place over medium–high heat. Add the spice paste and sauté for 2–3 minutes, stirring well. Add the bay leaves and vegetable stock, and bring to the boil. Add all the remaining ingredients except the peanuts, and mix well.

Bring back to a simmer, then reduce the heat and cook gently for about 15–20 minutes until all the vegetables are well cooked. Check the seasoning and add more salt or date syrup if needed. Add the peanuts to the broth.

Serve with cooked quinoa or rice, and add spoonfuls to the vegetable broth as you are eating.

1 teaspoon culinary/unflavoured coconut oil, or use good-quality vegetable oil (see page 13)

3–4 bay leaves

1.2 litres/quarts good-quality vegetable stock

large handful of fresh or frozen green/French beans, trimmed

2 large corn cobs/ears, cut into 5-cm/2-in. rounds

1 large or 2 small courgettes/zucchini, cut into 2.5-cm/1-in. pieces, or use squash

2 sticks of Chinese celery, trimmed and cut into thin 5-cm/2-in. batons

400 g/14 oz. white cabbage, cut into 5-cm/2-in. pieces

4–5 oyster mushrooms, roughly torn

2 large tomatoes, quartered

3 tablespoons tamarind pulp, or use 1½ teaspoons tamarind concentrate

1 tablespoon date syrup, or to taste, or use pure maple syrup or unrefined coconut sugar

1 teaspoon salt, or to taste

3 tablespoons red-skinned peanuts, lightly toasted

REMPAH/SPICE PASTE

6.5-cm/2½-in. piece of fresh galangal, peeled and finely chopped, or use fresh ginger plus 1 teaspoon freshly squeezed lemon juice

1 small red onion, quartered

1 small red Thai chilli/chile

4–5 large long red chillies/chiles

3 fat garlic cloves, or use 1 tablespoon garlic paste

4–5 macadamia nuts, or use 8–10 cashew nuts

1 teaspoon Korean fermented soybean paste/doenjang, or use brown or red miso paste

SERVES 4

INDONESIAN CORN 'RIBS'

4 large corn cobs/ears, or use
  frozen and fully defrosted
scant ½ teaspoon coriander seeds
scant ½ teaspoon cumin seeds
½ tablespoon extra-virgin coconut oil,
  or use culinary/unflavoured coconut
  or good-quality vegetable oil
  (see page 13)
1 small brown onion, finely chopped
2 fat garlic cloves, finely chopped,
  or use 2 teaspoons garlic paste
2.5-cm/1-in. thumb of fresh galangal,
  or use fresh ginger, peeled and finely
  chopped, or 1 heaped tablespoon
  galangal or ginger paste
2–4 small red Thai chillies/chiles,
  finely chopped, to taste, or use
  ½ tablespoon sambol olek
1 teaspoon ground turmeric
1 teaspoon salt, or to taste
1 large tomato, roughly chopped,
  or use ½ x 400-g/14-oz. can
  tomatoes, drained
3–4 tablespoons coconut cream,
  or use the thickest part of canned
  coconut milk
1 teaspoon date syrup, or use pure
  maple syrup or unrefined coconut
  sugar
1 lime
2 tablespoons red-skinned peanuts,
  toasted and roughly chopped
handful of freshly chopped coriander/
  cilantro
1 tablespoon desiccated/dried
  unsweetened shredded coconut,
  lightly toasted

baking sheet, lined with parchment

SERVES 4

Corn 'ribs' have become a bit of a social media sensation during the last few years, so I decided to give them an Indonesian twist. Barbequed/grilled corn cobs/ears are one of the most widely available street food snacks in Indonesia, even in the most remote areas.

We had been driving our way around the island of Lombok for a month, taking the coastal road clockwise from the capital Mataram on the west coast. With its scarcely used but well tarmacked roads, it's an incredibly easy place to self-drive and explore. We hiked up to mountain waterfalls and crater lakes, snorkelled the choppier reefs off the northern lava sand beaches and rested in homestays. Stopping for roasted corn (and watermelon) roadside snacks were often memorable moments in very remote areas. Big juicy cobs strung over the side of barbeque/outdoor grill barrels spluttered and sizzled. This was no drive-through moment, especially if there was sambal. Deliciously messy!

Preheat the oven to 220°C (425°F) Gas 7.

Using a sharp knife, slice the corn cobs/ears lengthways into quarters.

Place a frying pan/skillet over medium heat and add the coriander and cumin seeds. Lightly toast for 1 minute, then add half the coconut oil. Add the chopped onion to the pan and fry gently for 2 minutes, then add the garlic, galangal, chillies/chiles, turmeric and salt. Mix well and cook for a further 2 minutes.

Add the tomato and 2 tablespoons water. Bring to a simmer and cook over low heat for 5 minutes until the tomato has completely broken down. Add the coconut cream and date syrup, mix well and check the seasoning, adding more salt if needed.

Rub the corn ribs with the remaining oil and arrange them on the lined baking sheet. Place in the preheated oven and roast for 15–20 minutes until golden brown. (If you don't have whole corn cobs, you can simply add canned or frozen corn to the sauce and serve as a kind of corn curry.)

Using a zester, remove the rind from the lime, roughly chop it (not too fine) and set aside. Halve the lime and add 1 tablespoon of the juice to the sauce.

Pile up the (now curvy) corn ribs onto a big platter and drizzle with the sauce. Sprinkle with the toasted peanuts, fresh coriander/cilantro, coconut and lime rind. Serve immediately.

MANADO 'WOKU' CURRY

Manado is the capital city of the northern territory on the island of Sulawesi. It's also the hopping-off point for Bunaken National Marine Park, one of Indonesia's many spectacular diving and snorkelling sites. Like several other notable dive sites across this archipelago, it has some of the greatest diversity of marine life in the world. And some of the spiciest food!

Traditionally made with fish or chicken, this curry is distinctly Manadonese, with a very spicy rempah combined with fresh herbs and fragrant flavours. You can reduce the number of chillies/chiles if you prefer a less spicy version. This vegan version uses tempeh, but you can easily use firm tofu/beancurd or mock chicken, as well as any vegetables you have in the fridge.

Preheat the oven to 200°C (400°F) Gas 6.

Place the tempeh pieces onto the lined baking sheet and drizzle with the oil. Bake in the preheated oven for 20–25 minutes until starting to crisp and brown. Set aside.

Place all the ingredients for the rempah/spice paste into a blender or food processor and blitz until smooth. Pour the paste into a deep frying pan/skillet or wok and place over medium–high heat. Add the lime leaves, lemongrass, turmeric and pandan, if using. Bring to a simmer, then reduce the heat and cook for 6–7 minutes.

Add 500 ml/2 cups of water, the salt and date syrup. Mix well and bring back to a simmer over low–medium heat for 3–4 minutes until reduced slightly.

Add the tempeh pieces, green chillies/chiles, spring onions/scallions and tomato. Continue to cook for a few minutes until the spring onions/scallions are just softened. Remove from the heat and stir through the torn basil just before serving. Serve with steamed black rice and raw cucumber and mooli/daikon crudités on the side.

400 g/14 oz. tempeh, diced into 2.5-cm/1-in. pieces, or use firm tofu/beancurd or mock chicken
½ tablespoon culinary/unflavoured coconut oil, melted, or use good-quality vegetable oil (see page 13)
6–7 fresh or dried kaffir lime leaves
2 lemongrass sticks, heavily bruised
¼ teaspoon ground turmeric
10–12.5-cm/4–5-in. strip of pandan leaf (optional)
½–1 teaspoon salt, to taste
½ tablespoon date syrup, or use pure maple syrup or unrefined coconut sugar
7 large green chillies/chiles, sliced
2 spring onions/scallions, sliced
1 large tomato, cored and cut into wedges
large handful of freshly torn lemon basil, or use Italian basil plus 1 teaspoon lemon juice

REMPAH/SPICE PASTE
8 large red chillies/chiles, or use large dried chillies/chiles soaked in boiling water
2–4 Thai/small chillies/chiles, to taste
1 red onion, quartered
3 fat garlic cloves, or use 1 tablespoon garlic paste
5–6 candlenuts, or use 5–6 macadamia nuts or 10–12 cashew nuts
1 teaspoon ground turmeric, or use 2.5-cm/1-in. thumb of fresh turmeric root, peeled
2.5-cm/1-in. thumb of fresh ginger, peeled, or use 2 heaped tablespoons ginger paste
1 large tomato

TO SERVE
¼ cucumber, deseeded and cut into batons
¼ mooli/daikon radish, peeled and cut into batons

baking sheet, lined with parchment

SERVES 4

BALINESE-STYLE TAMARIND BRAISED AUBERGINES/EGGPLANTS
with savoury millet

This super-simple dish can be ready to eat in under 30 minutes, with easy-to-find ingredients. If you prefer a lower sugar content, substitute the kecap manis for soy sauce plus a little date syrup and extra spices, as this Indonesian condiment is usually high in sugar. Kecap (or ketjap) manis (sweet soy suace) is a sweet, thick, dark, molasses-like sauce made from reducing soy sauce and adding palm sugar/jaggery. It is also flavoured with aromatic spices. Indonesian lemon basil is a citrussy small-leafed basil, and can be hard to find. You could use a few lemon balm leaves, or a small squeeze of lemon juice with some Thai basil as a substitute. Serve with savoury millet for a healthy gluten-free option. Highly alkaline, it is packed with iron, potassium, B-vitamins and calcium.

Preheat the oven to 210°C (400°F) Gas 6.

Arrange the aubergine/eggplant pieces on the lined baking sheet and drizzle with half the oil. Bake in the preheated oven for 20–25 minutes until nicely browned. Set aside.

Rinse the millet in cold water, then toast it in a wide, deep frying pan/skillet over medium–high heat for 4–5 minutes. Add 530 ml/2¼ cups water, the vegetable stock powder/bouillon, salt and olive oil. Stir and bring to the boil, then reduce the heat, cover and simmer for 15 minutes, checking occasionally that it is not sticking. Remove from the heat, mix with a fork and replace the lid. Set aside for 10 minutes, fluff again with a fork and set aside.

Place a large wok or wide, deep frying pan/skillet over high heat and add the remaining oil and the sliced shallots. Turn down the heat to medium and sauté the shallots until just softening. Add the ginger and garlic, and stir-fry for 2 minutes. Add the aubergine/eggplant and all the remaining ingredients.

Mix well and add 125 ml/½ cup water. Bring to a simmer, then reduce the heat, cover and simmer for 10 minutes until the aubergines/eggplants are soft, but not completely falling apart.

Place the millet onto a large platter, add the braised aubergines/eggplants and top with a drizzle of yogurt and a scattering of herbs and toasted peanuts. Serve with some sambal balado.

2 aubergines/eggplants (about 500 g/1 lb. 2 oz.), tops removed and each sliced into 8 long wedges about 5–7.5 cm/2–3 in. thick
2 tablespoons culinary/unflavoured coconut oil, melted, or use good-quality vegetable oil (see page 13)
2 banana shallots, thinly sliced, or use 1 small brown onion
2-cm/¾-in. thumb of fresh ginger, peeled and finely chopped, or use 1 tablespoon ginger paste
3 fat garlic cloves, finely chopped, or use 1 tablespoon garlic paste
2 large red chillies/chiles, roughly chopped
4–5 fresh or dried kaffir lime leaves
3 tablespoons kecap manis/Indonesian sweet soy sauce, or use 3 tablespoons soy sauce plus 1 tablespoon date syrup or coconut sugar, 2 Indonesian long cloves and 1 star anise
80 ml/⅓ cup tamarind pulp (light brown unsweetened variety, do not use concentrate)
1 teaspoon salt, or to taste

SAVOURY MILLET
190 g/1 cup millet pearls/grains
1 heaped teaspoon good-quality vegetable stock powder/bouillon, or use 1 heaped tablespoon miso
½ teaspoon salt
1 tablespoon olive oil

TO SERVE
2 tablespoons coconut or vegan 'Greek-style' yogurt
handful of herbs, such as coriander/cilantro and Indonesian lemon basil
1 tablespoon red-skinned peanuts, lightly toasted
sambal balado (see page 197)

baking sheet, lined with parchment

SERVES 2–3

SAMBAL BALADO
Indonesian chilli/chile & tomato sambal

Spicy and flavourful sambal is a cornerstone of Indonesian food. There are numerous varieties of this much-loved condiment (a recent research count was 352 varieties of sambal across the archipelago), where some are raw (mentah) and some cooked (masak). The ubiquitous sambal bawang uses shallots and garlic, and is similar to Thai nam prik. Sambal balado includes tomato and lime, with sweet and zesty notes. This versatile recipe can be served alongside lots of other dishes, or even as a marinade.

10–12 large dried red chillies/chiles, to taste, soaked in boiling water for 15–20 minutes
2–6 Thai chillies/chiles, to taste (optional)
1 small red onion, roughly chopped
3 fat garlic cloves, or use 1 tablespoon garlic paste
1 large tomato, halved and deseeded
¼ tablespoon culinary/unflavoured coconut oil, or use refined olive oil or pomace oil
2–3 fresh or dried kaffir lime leaves (optional)
½ tablespoon date syrup, or to taste, or use pure maple syrup or unrefined coconut sugar
½–1 teaspoon salt, to taste
freshly squeezed juice of 1 lime

MAKES 250 ML/1 CUP

Drain the soaked chillies/chiles and add to a blender or food processor along with the fresh chillies/chiles (if using), onion, garlic and tomato. Blitz to a rough pulp, then add to a small pan with the coconut oil. Place over medium heat and bring to a simmer.

Add the lime leaves, date syrup and salt, and simmer gently for 10–12 minutes until the liquid reduces. Add the lime juice, mix well and taste. Adjust the seasoning, adding more date syrup or salt if needed.

Store in a sterilized jar and keep in the fridge for up to 2 weeks.

Above: Sun-dried chillies/chiles, Kopang street market, Lombok.

SATAY SILKEN TOFU/BEANCURD

1 tablespoon linseed/flaxseed meal mixed with 3 tablespoons cold water
4–5 tablespoons polenta/cornmeal, or use sesame seeds if you prefer
300 g/10½ oz. silken tofu/beancurd, carefully sliced into approx. 10 large oblong pieces
3 tablespoons culinary/unflavoured coconut oil, or use good-quality vegetable oil (see page 13)
1 small red onion, finely diced
2–3 fat garlic cloves, to taste, finely chopped, or use 2–3 teaspoons garlic paste
1 large red chilli/chile, finely chopped
120 g/4 oz. green/French beans, trimmed

SAUCE
3 teaspoons kecap manis/ Indonesian sweet soy sauce
2 teaspoons peanut butter
1 teaspoon chilli/chili sauce or sambol olek
½ teaspoon ground black pepper

TO SERVE
1–2 red chillies/chiles, to taste, thinly sliced at an angle
1 spring onion/scallion, thinly sliced at an angle
vegetable crudités
sambal balado (see page 197)

SERVES 2–3

This simple savoury dish is more popular in Indonesian homes than on restaurant menus. It's easy to prepare at home and can be served as a light meal or as part of an Indonesian mixed plate (aka nasi campur, see pages 179–180). Silken tofu/ beancurd is a very soft, versatile tofu/beancurd, sometimes called egg tofu/beancurd. Vegan cooks often use this as an egg replacement in baking. The crispy coated tofu/beancurd creates a deliciously contrasting texture to the soft custardy middle. You can substitute firmer tofu/beancurd, if you prefer, or even use assorted vegetables.

Place the linseed/flaxseed mixture into one bowl and the polenta into another. Carefully dip the tofu/beancurd pieces into the linseed/flaxseed mixture, and then coat in the polenta. Add half of the oil to a frying pan/skillet and place over medium–high heat. When the oil is hot, gently lay the coated tofu/beancurd pieces into the pan and fry for 8–10 minutes, carefully turning to brown on all sides. Once all sides are lightly browned, remove the pieces and set aside on paper towels.

Add the remaining oil to a clean frying pan/skillet and add the onion. Place over low–medium heat for 5 minutes until the onion is translucent. Then add the garlic and chilli/chile, cooking for a few more minutes.

Mix together all the sauce ingredients and then add to the onion mixture. Add 80 ml/⅓ cup of water to the pan and combine well. Bring to a simmer and cook for 1–2 minutes. Add the green/ French beans, cover the pan and cook for 3–4 minutes. Remove the lid and add 1–2 tablespoons water, if needed.

To serve, place the tofu/beancurd pieces onto a plate and pour over the satay mixture. Scatter with sliced chillies/chiles and spring onion/scallion. Serve with vegetable crudités and sambal on the side.

RAW PEACH
& PASSION FRUIT
'CHEESECAKE'

I never expected to see a dessert counter at a wellness retreat, and raw vegan cheesecakes were some of the most popular there. Inspired by the dessert counter at my favourite retreat, this recipe is lower sugar, lower carb and higher protein… and still tastes amazing!

After fasting for 8½ days and spending several days slowly reintroducing raw and lightly cooked food, I had been eyeing up the treat counter all week. With my birthday fast approaching, my new-found fasting friends and I planned a cake sharing party, so we could try all the flavours. Passion fruit and mango is the combo you're most likely to see, but we don't have widely available European mangoes. And even canned mango is hard to find in some countries (like Italy). Punchy passion fruit and sweet peach are an equally winning combination. And if passion fruits aren't in season, you can always use raspberries for the topping instead. Butterfly pea flower is incredibly rich in antioxidants and will add a vibrant colour to impress your guests.

BASE
95 g/1 cup rolled/old-fashioned oats
65 g/½ cup skinless almonds
40 g/½ cup desiccated/dried
   unsweetened shredded coconut
3 juicy, fat pitted dates (mejooli),
   or use 4–5 smaller dates
1 tablespoon extra-virgin coconut oil,
   or use culinary/unflavoured coconut
   oil or good-quality vegetable oil
   (see page 13)
large pinch of salt
1 teaspoon ground cinnamon
2 tablespoons unsweetened almond
   butter, or use cashew or peanut
   butter

FILLING
240 g/2 cups cashew nuts, soaked
   in cold water overnight and drained
½ x 400-g/14-oz. can coconut milk,
   thickest part only
450 g/2½ cups canned (in juice) or
   fresh peaches, puréed, or use mango
   if you prefer
1½ tablespoons agar agar,
   or alternative vegan gelatine
   (follow packet instructions)
80 ml/⅓ cup pure maple syrup
1 tablespoon freshly squeezed lemon
   juice
½ vanilla pod/bean, seeds removed,
   or use ½ teaspoon vanilla paste
   or 1 teaspoon pure vanilla extract
225-g/8-oz pack of vegan soft cheese
pulp and seeds of 1 passion fruit
2 teaspoons blue butterfly pea flowers,
   or use 1 teaspoon extract or
   ½ teaspoon powder (optional)

TOPPING
pulp and seeds of 4 passion fruit,
   or use 120 g/1 cup raspberries
1 heaped tablespoon black chia seeds
scant ¼ teaspoon agar agar
1 tablespoon freshly squeezed
   lemon or lime juice
½ tablespoon date syrup, or use
   pure maple syrup
handful of fresh, small edible pansies
   or violas, preferably purple, orange
   or yellow, to decorate (optional)

*20-cm/8-in. springform cake pan,
lightly oiled and lined*

SERVES 8–10

For the base, add the oats, almonds, coconut, dates, coconut oil, salt, cinnamon and almond butter to a food processor or blender, and blitz until a rough dough forms. Take care not to over-process; there should still be some visible nutty pieces. Press the dough into the lined cake pan, covering the bottom and using the back of a spoon to smooth the base. Place in the fridge for 30 minutes to set.

For the filling, add the soaked cashews to a food processor or blender, and blitz until smooth, adding a little of the coconut milk to achieve a really smooth consistency. Set aside.

Add the remaining coconut milk and peach purée to a small pan and add the agar agar, whisking quickly to avoid any lumps forming. Heat gently over low heat and continue to whisk until the mixture starts to simmer and thicken. Simmer gently for 3–4 minutes, whisking all the time. Remove from the heat and allow to cool slightly. Then add the mixture to the blender with the cashews, along with all the remaining filling ingredients (except the butterfly pea flowers),

and blitz until smooth and creamy. Pour half the mixture into the cake pan on top of the set base and smooth until even with the back of a spoon, tapping the pan to remove any air bubbles. Place in the freezer for 20 minutes.

Add the butterfly pea flowers (petal parts only) or pea flower extract or powder, if using, to the remaining mixture and blitz again until completely blended and smooth. Pour the remaining mixture into the cake pan, smoothing with the back of a spoon. Place back in the fridge and leave to set for 2–3 hours.

For the topping, scoop the passion fruit into a small pan. Add the chia seeds, agar agar, lemon juice, date syrup and 125 ml/½ cup water. Place over low heat, whisking to combine, and bring to a gentle simmer for a few minutes until the sauce is thickened.

Remove the cheesecake from the fridge, pour over the passion fruit mixture and use the back of a spoon to smooth the final layer. Cover the cake and place in the freezer for 2–3 hours, or in the fridge overnight.

Defrost the cheesecake at room temperature for at least 40 minutes before serving, or place in the fridge an hour before. Decorate the cake with edible flowers, if you like.

Above: Sun-dried butterfly blue pea flower, street market, Ubud, Bali.

HIBISCUS & GINGER KOMBUCHA

Kombucha has been taking the wellness world by storm for many years now, and we enjoyed some of our favourite versions in Indonesia. Kombucha is made from fermented tea that produces a powerful probiotic that supports gut health and immunity. It can be expensive to buy ready-made, so it's well worth learning to make your own. I buy my scoby 'mother' from a reliable online supplier for easy and safe brewing, but you can make your own if you have the time and patience (this can take between one and four weeks). You can keep using your scoby for every brew going forward. Once it becomes quite large, you can peel off a layer to create a second scoby, or share with your kombucha-loving friends!

There are a few essential kombucha-making rules, such as not using metal or plastic (use only glass jars or bottles for brewing). Everything must also be clinically clean to avoid any bad bacteria residues slipping into your brew. If you see any green, white or black mould (which is where using a ready-to-go scoby can help) then you will have to start again. The temperature of your environment will also make all the difference, so if it's cold, the process will be much slower.

Hibiscus has become a mainstay in my daily tea drinking because it's one of the most powerful natural remedies for high blood pressure. Recent studies have shown that four strong cups per day can deliver the same effects as Western blood pressure medicines. You can also add other flavours such as ginger, turmeric or any fruits you prefer (and omit the hibiscus). This recipe starts with a ready-made scoby, going through the first and second fermentations and creating flavours.

Dried hibiscus flowers,
Payangan market, Bali.

8 black tea bags
3–4 tablespoons dried hibiscus tea/
    flowers
160 g/1 cup coconut sugar,
    plus 8 teaspoons
1 kombucha scoby
5-cm/2-in. thumb of fresh ginger,
    peeled and thinly sliced

*4-litre/1-gallon glass jar with a wide
neck, sterilized
clean muslin/cheesecloth
rubber band
4–5 fermentation-grade flip-top
glass bottles, sterilized*

MAKES 4 LITRES/1 GALLON

First brew a big batch of sweetened tea by putting the tea bags, hibiscus and the 160 g/1 cup coconut sugar into a large, clean pan with 3.3 litres/14 cups water. (You can omit the hibiscus if you want to make plain kombucha and add some flavours at the next stage.) Bring to a simmer, then turn off the heat and leave to steep for 15–20 minutes.

Once fully cooled, you are ready to start the first fermentation. Pour your cooled tea into the glass jar. If you have not cooled this enough, you will kill your scoby, so be patient. With very clean hands, carefully place your scoby into the glass jar with the tea, adding up to 500 ml/2 cups of the liquid that the scoby was growing in. Cover the jar with the clean muslin/cheesecloth and wrap a rubber band around the jar neck to secure.

Set the jar in a dark place for 6–10 days. You want the average storage temperature to be around 21–24°C (70–75°F). After 6 days, you can check on your brew by using a straw to lift out a little of the liquid to taste. Do not use your mouth on the straw in the brew or double dip! It should taste slightly sweet and a little vinegary. The warmer the temperature the faster the ferment. And the longer the tea ferments, the more of the sugar is eaten up by the bacteria. I prefer to ferment for 9–10 days until the brew is much less sweet and more fermented.

When ready for the next stage, funnel the tea (using a clean scoop) into the sterilized glass bottles (you will need enough for about 4 litres/1 gallon) leaving at least a 7.5-cm/3-in. gap from the top of each bottle. Leave the scoby behind in the large glass jar with at least 500–750 ml/2–3 cups of the brew, and this will be your starter for the next batch. Add 3–4 ginger slices to each bottle, if using, and add 2 teaspoons of coconut sugar to each bottle. If you made your kombucha without hibiscus, you can add any other fruit flavour here, such as peach, pineapple, mango, strawberries or lemon, and these can replace the sugar at this stage if the fruit has a high-sugar content. You can also add herbs like mint or basil.

Seal the lid on each bottle and shake to mix. Set the kombucha bottles in a dark, warm place to ferment again for 3–10 days, depending on how warm the conditions are.

A word of warning here. The warmer the temperature, the faster the ferment, which means you need to keep a close eye on them and give them a burp every other day, or sometimes every day if it is warm. Not burping your bottles can cause kombucha explosions. Always point the top of the bottle away from your face (or any windows) as you flip the top to avoid any accidents. Prepare yourself for a big pop!

After this ferment, you can taste the brew again using the straw technique (not your mouth) and when you are happy with your fizz, you can transfer to the fridge, which will completely pause the fermenting process. The brews will keep for a month or two in the fridge.

When you are ready to drink, serve chilled from the fridge. Simply pour into a glass using a tea strainer.

Index

Reading list

Fischer, Louis, *Life of Mahatma Gandhi* (2004)

Him, Chanrithy, *When Broken Glass Floats* (2001)

Hirata, Andrea, *The Rainbow Troops* (2014)

Lapcharoensap, Rattawut, *Sightseeing* (2005)

Lewis, Norman, *A Dragon Apparent* (2003)

Mistry, Rohinton, *A Fine Balance* (1995)

Mistry, Rohinton, *Such A Long Journey* (1991)

Ninh, Bao, *The Sorrow of War* (2018)

Pamuntjak, Laksmi, *The Birdwoman's Palate* (2018)

Pramoj, Kukrit, *Four Reigns* (1998)

Rushdie, Salman, *Midnight's Children* (1981)

Trong Phung, Vu, *Dumb Luck* (2002)

Ung, Loung, *First They Killed My Father* (2006)